Psychic
Self
Defense

BY EMBROSEWYN TAZKUVEL

Celestine Light Magick Series

Angels of Miracles and Manifestation
144 Names, Sigils and Stewardships to Call the Magickal Angels of Celestine Light

Words of Power and Transformation
101+ Magickal Words and Sigils of Celestine Light to Manifest Your Desires

Celestine Light Magickal Sigils of Heaven & Earth

Secret Earth Series

INCEPTION *(Book 1)*
DESTINY *(Book 2)*

Psychic Awakening Series

CLAIRVOYANCE
TELEKINESIS
DREAMS

AURAS
How to See, Feel and Know

SOUL MATE AURAS
How Find Your Soul Mate & "Happily Ever After"

UNLEASH YOUR PSYCHIC POWERS

PSYCHIC SELF DEFENSE

LOVE YOURSELF
Secret Key To Transforming Your Life

22 STEPS TO THE LIGHT OF YOUR SOUL

ORACLES OF CELESTINE LIGHT
Complete Trilogy of Genesis, Nexus & Vivus

Published by Kaleidoscope Productions
1467 Siskiyou Boulevard, #9; Ashland, OR 97520
www.kaleidoscope-publications.com
ISBN 978-1494842673

Book layout and design by Sumara Elan Love
www.3wizardz.com

All rights reserved
This book including the cover illustration, may not be copied except sigils for personal use by the original purchaser. The book may not be reproduced or retransmitted by any means in whole or part, or repackaged, resold, or given away for free as a download, in whole or part, in any form.

Distribution
Only legally available to be purchased as a paperback book through retail or online bookstores, or in eBook format through major online retailers and their affiliates.

PLEASE DO NOT PARTICIPATE IN PIRACY.

PSYCHIC SELF DEFENSE

EMBROSEWYN TAZKUVEL

TABLE OF CONTENTS

Introduction..9

Part I: The Foundation
Chapter 1: Don't Give Energy to Fear.........................15
Chapter 2: Energy Shields...17
Chapter 3: Create an Auric Sphere of Power (ASP)......21
Chapter 4: Create an Energy Ward.............................29
Chapter 5: Quartz Crystal Shields..............................31
Chapter 6: Enchantments & Spells.............................37

Part II. Low Risk Threats
Chapter 7: Inexperience...45
Chapter 8: Mental & Emotional Garbage...................47
Chapter 9: Psychic Overload......................................51
Chapter 10: Empathy Overload..................................53
Chapter 11: Dismissive Opinions...............................55
Chapter 12: Negative Energy People.........................57
Chapter 13: Energy Dampening Locations................61
Chapter 14: Cleansing a Home of Negative Energy...63

Part III. Medium Risk Threats
Chapter 15: Entities & Blobs......................................73
Chapter 16: Scenes of Death & Destruction...............75
Chapter 17: Regretful Energy Vampires....................77

Part IV. High Risk Threats
Chapter 18: Disembodied Spirits & Haunted Buildings & Locations..85
Chapter 19: Alien Presence..91
Chapter 20: Demons..95
Chapter 21: Black Magic..105
Chapter 22: Wolf in Sheep's Clothing - Channeled...109
Chapter 23: Wolf in Sheep's Clothing - Human........113

Chapter 24: Predatory Energy Vampires..................121
Conclusion..125

INTRODUCTION

When you walk down the path of the psychic and paranormal, you are entering into a strange, wonderful new world where the limitations of the physical senses and the known laws of physics often do not apply. In this realm there are many unseen and unknown forces that can scare you at least, and hurt you at worst, if you are not prepared for them. Only the naive or inexperienced would doubt or deny this reality. However, there is nothing to worry or have anxiety about as long as you are aware of the risks and challenges and prepared to counter them.

I have been blessed to have been immersed in the psychic and paranormal world for almost 60 years now. I have had an incredible array and number of memorable experiences, from events as benign and wondrous as telepathy and miraculous healings, to as formidable and challenging as predatory energy vampires and malevolent demons.

For the last 18 years I have also been a full-trance, full-body channel for numerous higher beings, and have recorded several hundred hours in channel with everyone from Philos the Galactic to Miriam of Magdala. In the late 90's, I channeled several dozen different higher beings from the Celestine Order of Light (COOL), each with their own voice, personality, history and wisdom to impart. These included both male and female guides, as well as some that had never been in a human form and had challenging energies to full-body channel.

Based upon my deep and lengthy experience, I can state unequivocally that the practice of psychic self-defense is not something you should shrug off as "not necessary" or "no time for that." In addition to being a wise precaution, particularly when working with the energies of any other beings, be they ghosts, guides, or other off-world advisers, any time you practice any psychic ability, including self-defense, it strengthens and improves all of your psychic abilities.

In everyday life precautions become habits in direct proportion to the perceived threat. You don't leave your purse or wallet unattended in your shopping cart when you are browsing in a store. You don't park your car in public places with the doors unlocked, the windows rolled down and the keys left in the ignition. Nor do you walk down the street with cash hanging out of your pockets, or leave the door to your house wide open when you go on vacation. You guard yourself in ways commensurate with the risk, because you know if you don't there is a chance that something bad might happen. It is very much the same when you are working with psychic and paranormal activities. You take simple, common sense precautions to insure there is no chance of anything unpleasant or harmful occurring.

I've seen practitioners throw caution to the winds and as a matter of personal principle completely disregard self-defense. They feel it is somehow giving into fear and calling in the very energy trying to be avoided. That is an empowered and noble attitude. In the more benign psychic endeavors this carefree attitude is harmless because low level psychic activities offer little to no threat. But if followed through into the more risky psychic endeavors it will eventually end badly in one way or another.

Like so many things in life, balance is the key operative word. It is equally as unhelpful to disregard the risks, as it is to be paranoid and overly consumed by them. Reasonable precautions, especially with any psychic activity where supernatural beings of any kind are involved, is just common sense. When you are aware of the risks and are prepared to counter them, there is little likelihood you will ever need them.

The threat level is not the same for every paranormal/psychic activity. If you are using Biblioelucidation to receive an answer

Introduction

to a simple question the danger level is basically nil. But if you are channeling in another being, allowing them to enter and control your body in a trance, the risks are much higher. The best path is to be neither overly cautious or overly dismissive of the dangers. Consider wisely what the possible dangers may be for any psychic endeavor and take appropriate measures equal to the possible risks.

Truly, using supernatural abilities should be as pleasant as a walk in the park on a comfortably warm and serene summer's day. And it will be for you as long as you have your simple but effective psychic defenses prepared before you seek to explore your gifts too deeply. Too often people are so excited to learn and develop their psychic abilities and paranormal powers that they plunge into that aspect without caution or full awareness of dangers that may lie lurking. Learn and apply basic psychic defense procedures first and you will always have safe sailings on your supernatural journeys.

Embrosewyn Tazkuvel

PSYCHIC SELF DEFENSE

Introduction

PART I
THE FOUNDATION

PSYCHIC SELF DEFENSE

Chapter 1

DON'T GIVE ENERGY TO FEAR

Belief is very powerful. It affects how well you can call upon and use your special abilities. It also can aid or hinder you in your psychic self defense depending on whether you are defending yourself from a place of confidence and empowerment, or anxiety and fear. It is easy to give in to the latter. But I assure you that you have nothing to fear from the unseen world as long as you take the proper precautions. I am happy to share with you potent defenses I have proven work 100% of the time.

The First Defensive Step:

Never proceed with anything of a psychic or paranormal nature if you are fearful.

Your emotions are like psychic magnets. They call to you that which you strongly feel. If you feel fear, those forces that feed on fear are drawn to you. If you feel confident and empowered, the forces that feed on fear are repelled. Fear is a darkness. When you have fear you call more darkness to you. Self-confidence and personal empowerment are light. Darkness cannot exist in the presence of light.

The Second Defensive Step:

Do not associate with people who are fearful when you are involved in psychic activities.

Fear draws more fear. A fearful group of people draw an exponentially larger amount of fear and darkness. Both in the visible and unseen worlds, there are people, beings, forces and sundry energies that are empowered and drawn to people who are negative and fearful. The fears of those people and the darkness they draw to them can rub off on you when you are in their presence, especially when jointly involved in a psychic activity.

Chapter 2

ENERGY SHIELDS

Energy shields come in two varieties. The first type are constructed purely of energy, usually a combination of your own auric energy, plus universal energies you draw in from points beyond to buttress and further empower the shield. Psychic Energy Shields will be explained in detail directly below.

The second type is also energetic in nature and creation, but has its power expanded and maintained for longer periods of time by imbuing the energy inside a special physical receptacle/amplifier, such as a quartz crystal. Quartz crystals are potent and primary physical amplifying shields. Their use is explained in detail in the following chapter. Other techniques utilizing different types of physical energy amplifiers will be explained on a case-by-case basis in the sections on "Threats."

The First Energy Shield:

Visualize and encircle yourself with a protective dome of sparkling golden-white light.

Look at the cover of this book for a moment. Similar to the brilliant white light radiating out from the empowered woman on the cover, preface your psychic and paranormal activities by first creating a sphere of shimmering, golden-white light surrounding and protecting you. You are the master. Set the parameters of your protective dome of light that no darkness, person, being or entity that would harm you can pass its protective walls.

Inside your golden-white sphere of protective light you are safe. It moves with you as you walk or travel from place to place.

You can create it in the morning when you awaken and empower it with your belief throughout the day. You can create another or reinforce the one from the morning just before you sleep to protect you at night. If you are preparing to conduct a specific psychic task you can strengthen it again. To those who have never experienced the unseen world this may seem like a silly game. But to those who have, the golden-white sphere of light has proven to be a very effective shield.

Whether you choose to have more gold or more white light, or even all gold or all white, should be dictated by your own inner promptings directing you to the choice that is best for you at that time.

The Second Energy Shield:

*In situations where the threat is greater, empower your golden-white light sphere
with auric energy.*

Your aura is an astoundingly powerful force. Not only does it well up from the very essence of your soul, you have the ability through it, to call in all kinds of wonderful reinforcing and supporting energies from near and far beyond. Your aura can repel physical people as well as disembodied spirits, otherworldly entities and all forms of dark or negative energy.

Its ability to repel people is easily seen with any person whether they are psychically attuned or oblivious. Whenever anyone stands face to face to speak with another person, they only stand as close to them as is comfortable for both people. This distance differs from person to person and it is not related to whether they know them or not.

If you randomly met 10 unknown people and engaged them in conversation, with most you would be comfortable speaking to them while standing about 2 feet away. Some you could stand closer to and it would feel fine. While standing that close to others among the 10 would make both you and them feel uncomfortable.

Energy Shields

Why? Because you are pressing against the space where they have unconsciously set their auric shield, and though unseen, it is a very firm wall. If you try to approach them closer, they will actually take a step back to maintain the distance they have unconsciously set for their safety and comfort zone. If their back is to a wall and they cannot back up they will step to the side. If they are in a corner and can neither back up or step aside, they will get unexpectedly agitated if you approach too close, like a scared dog trapped in a corner. Try it out at the next group gathering you attend. The results are reliably predictable.

Chapter 3

CREATE A PROGRAMMABLE AURIC SPHERE OF POWER (ASP)

The easiest way to focus your auric energy is between your hands. This is something you can physically feel within a few seconds. Close your eyes, rub your hands together vigorously for a few seconds, then clap them soundly once. Then hold your hands, palms facing each other about 1 foot apart. Now slowly bring them closer together. You will feel a thickening of the space between your hands. Some people feel a tingling or a hot or cold sensation. You may feel all of those! When your hands are almost touching, move them slowly apart. Repeat this opening and closing motion multiple times. You will become more sensitive to the thickening, tingling, hot/cold physical feeling of your auric energy between your hands with every in and out movement.

The concentration of auric energy between your hands can be shaped, molded and programmed to do a variety of tasks. Usually practitioners of the psychic arts call this a 'psi ball.' When applied to psychic defense, I prefer 'Auric Sphere of Power.' This abbreviates as ASP, which is the name for a family of highly venomous snakes including the deadly Egyptian Cobra. I like to envision empowering my golden white sphere of light with focused, intentioned auric energy. The subsequent ASP that reinforces and strengthens my golden sphere protects me from all harm or negativity, like a circle of golden Egyptian Cobras.

Types of ASPs

Decide what type of ASP you are going to create. These fall into 4 categories:

A. **Mirror ASP:** A mirror ASP simply reflects back whatever harmful energy is trying to pass through your golden sphere. For the intruder, this can be a fairly benign and painless defense. Or, it can be painful. It depends upon the type of intrusion.

If your intention was to keep certain people away, such as those with negative attitudes, the result would be their negativity would bounce back at them. If they were intending to speak with criticism toward you, or about someone else, they would instead find they suddenly became mired in critical thoughts of themselves.

If someone were actually sending a psychic attack of any kind against you, a Mirror ASP would return the energy to the sender and hit them with whatever pain they were intending to cause you.

Mirror ASP's get stronger as needed when they are attacked. Because it is directly tied to your aura and energies beyond that it coalesced, the more it is attacked, the more energy it calls to the defense. As some of that energy is from universal sources, it is boundless and limitless. If you are protected by a Mirror ASP and someone is intentionally trying to hurt you with any type of psychic energy, they can become completely exhausted, even to the point of illness, by their fruitless efforts. Once the attack ceases, the Mirror ASP will soon return to a minimal, almost unnoticeable level of basic defense energy.

If you use a Mirror ASP, it is important when you

construct and shape it between your hands that you command that any energies repelled are always returned to the sender. If you leave this crucial little bit out, the Mirror ASP will reflect the energy randomly. You will be protected, but other innocent people nearby may be hit and hurt by the reflection.

Mirror ASP's are my favorite. I have no desire to hurt another person or any other thing that might be trying to hurt me. But if they are injured by their own dark intent, simply because I chose to not be a victim and to protect myself...so be it.

B. Absorb ASP: If you really want to be nice to those dark forces that are not trying to be sweet to you, you can use an Absorb ASP. Negative psychic energies that hit the wall of your golden sphere are simply absorbed and neutralized. No harm to you, no harm to the attacking person or forces.

When you create your ASP between your hands, before you enlarge it into a protective sphere, remember to specify that it is an Absorb ASP if that is your intention.

I have found that using Absorb ASP's except for short durations when they are the best choice for specific challenges, can be stifling. When harmful energies hit the walls of an Absorb ASP, they are neutralized and absorbed into the shield. If you are being attacked over time by many dark energies, the weight of the energy being retained by the Absorb ASP can become heavy and burdensome, interfering with your thoughts and actions simply by it's 'too heavy to ignore' oppressive weight.

If you ever find this to be the case, reverse your construct. Using your hands, visualization and intent, pull in the Absorb ASP until it is once again contained within the space between your two hands. Vocally thank it for its good service, then release it and dissipate it.

If you are still in need, simply create another Absorb ASP that will not yet be oppressive because it holds excessive energy from attacks.

C. Transmute ASP: Energy cannot be destroyed, but it can be changed into another form that is unusable for its intended purpose. This is exactly what a Transmute ASP does. The results can be unexpected and quite consequential, which is why this type should only be attempted and utilized by experienced practitioners who are well versed in ASP control.

The construction of the ASP is similar to the Mirror and the Absorb, except your intention, which you vocalize, is to create a Transmute ASP. Harmful energy directed at you will not be reflected or absorbed, but instead changed into a form of energy that cannot negatively affect or harm you.

D. Multilayered ASP: I mention this type of ASP, even though constructing it will be beyond the abilities of all but those most experienced in use of their psychic and paranormal powers. This is really a type of punishment ASP. If someone or something has really been bothering you with ceaseless attacks of negative or dark energy and they haven't been deterred by their lack of success, it may be time to use a Multilayer ASP in your defense. It's like having a mosquito continuing to buzz and try to bite you despite all the benign defenses you have presented. When a mosquito seems to not care that you are sending it love, seems to be unaffected by all your golden light, and still lands on you and lowers it proboscis to suck your blood, it's time for a fatal swat! It is similar when you reach a point of frustration at continuing to be attacked despite your more benign efforts to protect yourself.

If you are tempted to use a Multilayer ASP, that means you have already tried Absorb and Mirror ASP's, and maybe a Transmute ASP. While they have protected you,

Create a Programmable Auric Sphere of Power

they have failed to stop the attacks.

The most effective Multilayer ASP is to combine a Mirror with a Transmute. When dark psychic energy is hurled at you the Mirror will reflect it back to the sender. Remember however, that because it is coupled with a Transmute, it will return in a different form, that may affect the sender in unknowable, uncontrollable, significant and consequential ways. Because of this, it is vitally important that you insure that the energy returns only to the sender and can in no way accidentally be off course and injure anyone else. State this clearly when you create the Multilayered ASP.

Though you can try to control and set the type of energy that the original energy will transmute into, there is no way to do this with a certain degree of success. There is so much even the most advanced practitioners do not know. When energies transmute from one form into another, they do it based upon their own natural laws, which are numerous. It's like planting what you think is an orange seed, only to see a grapefruit tree appear. Or, even worse, a thorn bush.

When you are dealing with people, there are some who actually thrive on negativity. If they send you negative energy and it bothers and affects you, knowing that feeds them and they are happier. If you create a mirror shield that reflects the negative energy back to them, it just replenishes their supply and once again they are happy. However, if you use a Mirror and a Transmute to send altered energy back to them, it may affect them or change them in ways neither of you may want. They may go from an overbearing negative @&)*&% to a useless wimpy personality. The consequences of energy transformation can be that severe!

How to Create an ASP

1. Begin by forming the auric ball of power between your hands as previously described.
2. Sit in a chair with a small table between your legs, or the corner of a larger table that comes about to knee height or a bit taller. If you are creating a mirror ASP, place a hand mirror 6-12 inches in diameter on the table. If you are creating an Absorb ASP, place a large natural sponge on the table instead of the mirror. If you are creating a Transmute ASP, place two dissimilar objects on the table such as a coin and a flower. If you are creating a Multilayered ASP, place the corresponding items representing the ASP on the table.
3. Form your auric ball of power between your hands while looking down at the representative objects just below your hands. Whatever it is you need your ASP for, put that intention into the energy sphere between your hands.
4. State aloud, "I am forming a (type of ASP) to (fill in specifically the purpose of the ASP.)
5. Continue by saying, "I form this (type of ASP) with my own auric energy. I am connected to it and it to me."
6. Continue by saying, "I call upon all the energies of might and light to further empower this (type of ASP) to reflect away all (fill in specifically the purpose of the ASP.) As you say this look upward. See in your mind or with your psychic eyes a brilliant, golden white light beaming down upon you in a massive sparkling column of light from far in the heavens above. Allow the light to enter you and fill every cell of your body with its power. Visualize your body glowing and radiating the golden white light from every pore. Feel the energy of the light swirling inside of you. Concentrate it within your body. Then send it with your mental command and intent down your arms,

Create a Programmable Auric Sphere of Power

shooting out the palms of your hands and immensely empowering your ASP.

7. Now pull your hands apart and see and feel the ASP retaining its shape, but getting larger and larger until it reaches the size you want it to be. Determine how big you want your ASP to be and visualize, manipulate and command it to be so. This may be as small as the personal space near your body that moves with you as you walk or travel, to as large as your home. Or perhaps you are in a room or even a home with other people working together on a psychic project and you need the entire space protected.

8. Pull your hands apart as you expand the size of the ASP. Once it is the size of your outstretched arms, begin a series of pushes with your palms facing out, until you have pushed your ASP outward far enough that it is encompassing the area of protection you desire. I also always envision the outer perimeter wall of the ASP to be full of ghostly, white or golden cobras reared up, with their hoods spread, ready to protect me as needed.

9. See the space between you and the wall of the ASP completely filled with light. Now draw your own aura back close to your body and see the space between you and the walls of the ASP become normal transparent space. Your aura is now back close to you, but the walls of the Auric Sphere of Protection, your ASP, are still visible, scintillating golden white light and alive with the energy in which you and the universe endowed it. Your ASP is now complete and on duty.

SPECIAL NOTES:

1. The larger the size of the ASP, the more diffused its energy. The smaller the size, the more concentrated and potent its energy. If you need to pump up the power of your ASP for a room or house, add quartz crystals as

described further below in the section on Demons.

2. You should spend about 5 minutes each day repeating steps 7-9 to recharge and revitalize your auric energy shield, especially if you know it has taken some blows of negativity. ASP's work best when they are not used for too long of time. The power of the energy field you create does diminish as time passes unless it is regularly being restrengthened.

3. You can choose to restrengthen and renew your golden ASP sphere periodically through focused intention, visualization and vocalized commands. Or, you can simply deconstruct it by using intent and visualization, along with inward movements of your hands and arms, to pull the energy sphere back until it is once again contained within the space between your hands. Once there, simply thank it for its service and dissipate it with an opening movement of your hands and your intent.

Chapter 4

CREATE AN ENERGY WARD

ASPs are effective, active shields against all forms of negative or dark energy and should be in your standard psychic tool kit. But what about when you need something extra potent, whose positive energy will dissipate more slowly than an ASP sphere? A Ward is the answer. Think of 'ward off' or 'keep away' when you think about Wards. Wards are a noxious energy to anyone or anything you have created them to repel.

Wards are constructed the same way ASPs are made: with your intention, vocalization and formed between your hands. Unlike the general defense of an ASP, with their large golden sphere of protection, Wards keep their energy concentrated in a small area, or in a larger area but with a single defined purpose. Existing for a focused, singular purpose, their energy lasts a long time; easily for days and often for weeks, or even months, before it weakens and dissipates.

You can also construct Wards for the benefit of other people as long as you place them in a location around the other person where they are needed. A good example is spiders. If you or someone you were creating a Ward for, cringed at the thought of the annual winter migration of spiders from outside to inside the house as the weather turns cold, an anti-spider Ward would solve the problem. Just use your visualization and movements of your hands and arms to create and place the Ward in a centrally located part of a room to protect, such as a bedroom, and you'll have no unwanted spider visitors in that room as long as the energy of the Ward remains.

Chapter 5

QUARTZ CRYSTAL SHIELDS

While a positive approach to life and avoidance of negative energy people and places remains your best defense, it is not foolproof, and it is possible you could still come under intentional psychic attack by disembodied beings or someone utilizing black magic. If you feel someone has cursed you, or that you are under any type of intentional psychic attack from living people or disembodied beings, you can create an impenetrable barrier of energy to protect yourself with quartz crystals. This shield is very effective against virtually all types of negative energy; and in many instances even against physical attack.

You will need to purchase 4 fist size quartz crystals for use around your bed, another 4 for use in your bedroom, and 4 additional crystals for every room you wish to always be protected within. Smaller crystals can work as well, but with less of a power output to the shield. Both size and clarity are important when using quartz crystals for protective purposes. The less clarity it has, the larger size is needed. Conversely, the greater clarity it has, the smaller size is needed.

You can find a wonderful assortment of quartz crystals that you can order online by simply doing a search for "Arkansas Quartz Crystals." Buying direct from the quartz crystals mines with their small minimum order requirements, is always far less expensive than buying from any retail outlet. Two of the biggest

The picture above shows two quartz crystal pendants.

in Arkansas are the Coleman Brothers in Jessieville. Jim and Ron own separate mines and run separate businesses right across the road from each other. Both have amazing quartz crystals in astounding quantity. But there are several other excellent mine outlets between Jessieville and Mt. Ida that have huge assortments of great crystals at very reasonable prices. If online buying isn't for you and you want to feel the energy of the crystals you buy, that area of Arkansas, centered around the picturesque town of Hot Springs, and the National Park of the same name, is quite beautiful and makes a very memorable road trip.

You will also need a single quartz crystal pendant of exceptional clarity to wear around your neck. The power of your overall crystal security system will be at least doubled if not more, by having the pendant around your neck in a setting of at least 14kt gold. 18kt. is superb. Gold is a fabulous conductor of positive energy. The crystals laid out in four corners with a fifth personal crystal around your neck, create a laser-like lattice

Quartz Crystal Shields

of white energy that any negative manifestation of darkness will not cross.

Both have special properties that make them even more effective. The crystal on the left is on an 18 kt gold chain encased in a custom-made 18 kt gold setting. The higher purity of the gold the more effective it is at extending the length of time the quartz crystal energy lattice maintains full power.

The crystal itself is a natural, unpolished, double-terminated crystal with a scepter on the larger end. Double terminated crystals are great for keeping energy balanced. When used with a quartz crystal grid they are very effective at maintaining uniform energy throughout the grid so there are no weak areas. Scepters are magnificent amplifiers of energy.

The pendant on the right has an extra large scepter which increases its ability to amplify the power of the quartz crystal grid. The pendant on the right also has an accompanying natural gold nugget with a diamond. Gold nuggets tend to be around 22 kt. Gold, which just further enhances the strength of the energy grid. The diamond embedded in the gold nugget calls in additional energy from the earth and heavens.

All of these special features can be seen in the auras created by the pendants and the quartz crystal energy shield.

To Empower, Program, Sync And Activate Your Crystal Shield

1. Take all the crystals you will be using, including your quartz crystal pendant and gold chain and wash them thoroughly in a warm bath of salt water. Scrub off any dirt with a soft tooth brush and let them soak in a plastic tub of salt water for at least 24 hours. Metal tubs and bowls should be avoided as they may react with the salt water and alter its composition.
2. After 24 hours discard the water, refill with fresh salt water and let set for another 24 hours.
3. If you do not have natural water from the ocean readily available you can make your own salt water. Add ½ cup

of natural, uniodized sea salt to every gallon of reverse osmosis or distilled water.

4. The water should be preheated to approximately 80 degrees Fahrenheit (comfortably warm). To avoid internal fracturing, the crystal should also be within 10 degrees of the same temperature when it is placed in the water. If you have a small submersible water pump to maintain a flow of water movement within the tub that would be also be helpful; otherwise stir with a long-handled wooden spoon about once per hour while you are awake.

5. Let the water sit overnight, heat to 80 degrees again the next day, and stir the water vigorously.

6. After your crystals have soaked for 24 or more hours, remove them and let them air dry in a very sunny location where they are in direct contact with the bare ground. Leave them in the direct sun for as long as possible during the day. Bring them in once the sun is no longer on them. They are now ready to program for your protection.

7. Find any object that you can easily hold that represents divinity as you know and believe. This can be a crucifix for a Christian, a Star of David for those who are Jewish, the pentacle for Wiccans, the Tri-circle of Twelve Gems for practitioners of Celestine Light, or any symbol or emblem that draws you and calls you to the divine. If you have no belief in any divine or higher source, the crystal lattice shield will still work in most instances. But against a very strong psychic or demon attack it will crumble, unless you have imbued it with a very powerful, confident energy of your own. Imbuing it with a connection to the divine reinforces it with energy that is not only powerful, but also repugnant and repelling to demons and other creatures and people of darkness.

Quartz Crystal Shields

8. Cradle all of your crystals in your arms held against your chest, along with the symbol of divinity you have chosen.
9. Say the following prayer/incantation to program and encode the crystals for their purpose: *Into these crystals birthed of Mother Earth, I call upon all energies of light to imbue with power to forever repel any and all energies or beings of darkness that would try to pass.* The more passion and conviction you say this with, the more potent the energy shield becomes.
10. (Optional) If you are a believer in any form of the divine, you should also call upon the god or gods of your belief to charge the crystals with their power and light to *forever repel any and all energies or beings of darkness that would try to pass.*
11. Now set one crystal at each of the four corners of your bed and another four at each of the four corners of your bedroom. The placement can be on the floor at the base of the bed legs, or if your bed is on a raised platform you can set them on the platform by the corners of the bed. It you have an odd shaped room, set a crystal in every corner. Your bedroom is now super protected.
12. If there are any other rooms you wish to protect, place a crystal in each corner of the room. If you want to protect your entire house, you can place a crystal outside or inside at each corner of the house.
13. If there is more than 20 feet distance between crystals, you should place another in between to shorten the distance. This strengthens the protective shield.
14. Wear your crystal pendant on a necklace. This strongly connects your aura to the energy lattice field of the crystals.

Chapter 6

ENCHANTMENTS & SPELLS

There's a lot of misconception when it comes to enchantments and spells. Some people feel they are evil by nature, others think only people immersed in witchcraft can cast them. While some spells and enchantments can be fairly complex, many others are simple yet still quite potent and powerful, and can be created by anyone with desire and a willingness to follow the simple steps outlined here.

I have always considered spells as a form of concentrated prayer. You may or may not be praying to a deity, but you are making a prayer of power that is laser focused on a singular goal. Whether in writing or speech, people by nature tend to be overly wordy. They have an inability or unwillingness to state their thoughts and desires concisely. Yet it is the very act of being concise that sharpens the focus upon the task at hand. The sharper the focus the greater the effect, because every bit of energy expended is utilized more productively.

An apt comparison would be between a light bulb and a spell. (Don't laugh it really is a good comparison.) The old incandescent light bulbs are only 10% efficient; 90% of their energy is wasted and expelled as heat; only 10% actually creates light. The newer LED bulbs use 60% of their energy to create light and only waste 40% in heat, which is why they are more efficient and a better purchase for your money. Similarly, if you are trying to achieve any objective just wishing it would happen, like the incandescent bulb you are wasting at least 90% of your energy, which is why wishes seldom come true. But if you craft a spell, the effort required to concisely encapsulate your desire in a handful of words that rhyme and have synergy with one another, is a powerful tool of focus in its own right. A far greater percentage of your energy is applied to manifesting your desire. Even if you say a spell written by someone else, if it is well-crafted, its concise and harmonious nature will still ensure a far greater likelihood of success. Once you reach the point that you are writing your own spells their power and effect are multiplied even more.

A really great free site to help you find rhymes is
www.rhymezone.com

I have been crafting spells to create enchantments and coalesce specific energies for several years, particularly for defensive purposes. They have proven to be particularly effective in certain situations. Occasionally people write asking me to create a spell for them. Instead, I usually try to help them craft their own. However, there was an incidence a couple of years ago where I gave in and wrote the spell and cast the enchantment after repeated pleas from a desperate man.

I first received an inquiry via email from Matt, explaining that he had a neighbor lady on his cul de sac, that had cursed him two weeks prior when he went to retrieve his dog from her garden. He said initially he disregarded her as just kooky. But after two weeks of suffering horrible illnesses and accidents he had concluded the curse was the real cause and wrote to me wanting to know if there was any way I could counter the curse.

I tried to guide him to understand how to help himself, but things were not getting better and he was getting more and more frantic in his communications. My problem with his dilemma is I only had his word for the cause. I didn't want to coalesce any type of energy that would automatically negatively affect his neighbor lady, because there might not be a curse involved at all; it might just be his imagination! He might just be sick and accident prone.

I finally settled on an equitable solution and asked Matt to mail one of his silver rings to me that fit his finger and he could

Enchantments & Spells

wear, which I would enchant for him to counter the curse. I warned him that the process of casting the enchantment would change the color of the ring and it would no longer appear silver. He was OK with that and express mailed a ring to me.

Once his ring was in hand, I crafted a spell to enchant the ring with a powerful mirror ASP energy; one specifically designed to repel any curses sent his way. All he would need to do would be to wear the ring continually. If his problems really were from a curse, they would soon alleviate. If the lady down the street had truly cursed him, she would soon begin suffering the very same traumas Matt perceived he was being inflicted with. If she was not the source of his problems, she would suffer no ill effects from the enchantment.

It wasn't long after he received the ring back in the mail that I began hearing of good results back from Matt. A few days after he started wearing the ring he emailed that he had not had a single accident since he put the ring on and all of his medical issues had quickly cleared up. The most amazing email came two weeks after he had been wearing the ring. He wrote to tell me that the "witch" had moved out of her house in the dead of the night and he awoke in the morning to find her and all of her belongings completely gone. No one ever found out what happened to the "witch" or where she vanished to, but Matt never again suffered the problems of his curse.

You can write a spell for just about anything as a means to more greatly focus the needed energy on the desired task or goal. And you don't need to be a practicing witch or wizard. The foundation is simply a matter of crafting the best rhyme you can that succinctly expresses your desires. Please keep in mind that a 'white magic' spell is one where you are not using the spell to exert your will or desires upon an unsuspecting person. For that reason, though love spells are popular, they are often not ethical. If you are using a spell, that is not a defensive spell, to compel a person to an action they would not otherwise take that is 'black magic.' You could still craft a love spell if it was only about you-to make yourself have more self-confidence, or appear more radiant or desirable. Those type of actions are all benign 'white magic' and can effectively be used as love spells.

Of course, if it is a defensive spell against someone that is attacking you, psychically, mentally, emotionally, or physically, spells to repel the attacks, even if they involve compulsion, are just.

Here are a couple of examples: of how rhyme works to help concisely state the goal and thereby coalesce and focus the needed energy.

This is a spell we crafted on the fly in 2006. My wife and I had just left on a 45 minute trip to get to a ferry that was departing in 20 minutes. We had to make that ferry. A very important engagement waited for us on the other side of the water. We realized that even if we risked a ticket and sped, there was no way we could make the ferry in time. It was only a few seconds after that realization that we knew our only hope was a very potent time spell; so as we drove we crafted. We also realized we were going to need a little extra help and decided to ask for assistance in the spell from the Angel of Time.

Here's the spell we wrote and cast while we drove. And yes, we did catch the ferry. It didn't depart late and we didn't speed (much), but time certainly compressed.

> *We call upon Chronos, Angel of Time,*
> *to come to us, hear our rhyme.*
> *On our journey to the ferry,*
> *let us make now, oh so merry.*
> *Compress the minutes as we travel.*
> *Normal time, let us unravel.*
> *As we command, so let it be.*
> *From this very moment, blessed be!*

Here is a spell we crafted in May 2007. We were scheduled to speak at an event that was expecting potential disruptions from

Enchantments & Spells

people opposed to the purpose of the group. We required peace and harmony for the success of our project, so crafted this spell for that particular event. Once again, we called in assistance from heavenly forces.

We call upon celestial powers on high
to hear our words, and with sureness reply.
Upon a trip to Seattle we soon embark
keep us safe within a shielding energy ark.
Place a barrier around us to protect,
no harm to come, all evil to deflect.
Let any who would bother us,
be turned away, their plans made dust.
Upon the angels one and all we call,
stand for us, make evil fall.
This we command, this we decree.
By the power of the light,
so let it be.

Here is another that was cast as an enchantment upon a ring, as was done for Matt. In this case, the person had terrible self-confidence and it was hurting them in many ways in their life from relationships, to school, to work. The purpose of the enchantment was to insure that all energies supportive of self-confidence coalesced and continued to swirl around the wearer of the ring.

We call upon the Celestine powers of confidence,
to be drawn into this ring of gold, oh so intense.
Within this beautiful ring let confidence brim,
that upon the wearer it will never dim.
We command the energy of confidence held within the ring
to flood her aura and great poise and sureness bring.
May this talisman always be true,

within the wearers heart let it ever renew.

This we decree, this we command,

with the power of the light, let the energy expand.

One very important aspect you should notice about spells is that they are said with an attitude of empowerment and command, not weakness or subservience. Though angels and God may be called upon, it is done not from an attitude of pleading for help, but from a position of empowerment that simply calls on higher forces, knowing they will come, and commanding not asking for the necessary energies to flow. Attitude in both the words spoken and the tone and manner they are spoken has a HUGE effect on whether the spell or enchantment will be fully empowered to serve you as you desire.

PART II
LOW RISK THREATS

Following in the next three sections of the book is a comprehensive but not exhaustive list, of many of the threats and pitfalls that can be experienced by all who venture into the psychic and paranormal world. They are grouped as 'low risk', 'medium risk', and 'high risk.' Remember, this is a listing of risk or threat to your physical, mental, psychic, or emotional well-being. In the low risk category there are irritations that are not listed, that may temporarily discombobulate you and make it difficult or impossible to use your psychic abilities, but they are not usually dangers to your safety.

PSYCHIC SELF DEFENSE

Chapter 7

INEXPERIENCE

The first obstacle is simply inexperience. Often an inexperienced practitioner will be frightened by something they see, hear, or intuit psychically, simply because it was completely unlike anything in their prior experience. Strange and unusual doesn't make it bad or dangerous. The unknown is frequently frightening or disquieting, even in everyday life. If you are walking on a dark night and see a shadow flit by, it can cause a lot of anxiety. But as soon as you observe that it was caused by a swaying branch or something else identifiable and non-threatening, your anxiety and fear vanish.

It is the same when developing your psychic and paranormal abilities. On your journey of psychic/paranormal exploration you will encounter far more that is new to your experience than you do in your everyday life. In this regard, knowledge is truly power. The more you learn about those psychic and paranormal powers that you are interested in and drawn to, the less unpleasant surprises you will have. The more you know, the less you will misinterpret benign manifestations as threatening. The more you know, the more you will grow.

Chapter 8

MENTAL AND EMOTIONAL GARBAGE

As we go through life we all experience unpleasant and sometimes traumatic experiences that negatively affect us throughout the rest of our lives until we purge them. Think about it as taking out the mental and emotional trash. The longer you wait to take out the trash, the more it builds up and stinks up your life. Many people just cover the refuse of life up with an out-of-sight, out-of-mind attitude. But no matter how much you bury the memories, they are still there putrefying inside of you until you cleanse yourself of them. You may think the refuse is gone, until something triggers the memory and all of the bad thoughts and painful emotions come rushing back. You have to literally take out and remove the trash if you want to insure it doesn't keep returning from time to time to sink you into a morass. You cannot allow mental and emotional garbage to remain active within the house that is your life and expect it not to affect the quality of your life; especially if you continue to just add more garbage to the pile and never act to remove it.

Every negative experience you have ever had was a life lesson. But once it has been experienced and the lesson learned, it becomes refuse to remove or energetically neutralize. A more agreeable way to think of the process is as emotional and mental cleansing. From the person you didn't even know that vented their anger on you, to the date that stood you up, to the grief you suffered at the loss of a loved one from separation or death, to the big regret that keeps causing you grief, to the over demanding boss or the demeaning spouse, from a dog bite to a really bad Monday morning, all of us have negative experiences on a regular basis. The negative mental memories and the emotional residue left behind by these experiences are the garbage that must be purged or neutralized on a regular basis, until doing so becomes an unconscious good habit of mental and emotional housecleaning.

This is not simply for your own mental and emotional well-being. Your ability to mount stout psychic defenses is weakened if you are in an upset state mentally or emotionally. This is true even for subconscious thoughts and emotions that you have buried inside and outwardly forgotten about. If they haven't been negated, then they are still percolating inside and insidiously hindering you. Any negative thoughts or feelings you are experiencing or have experienced and buried inside are your enemies. Hatred, jealousy, anger, frustration, regret, or any other emotional pain or mental stress, not only weakens your psychic defenses, it also inhibits all of your psychic abilities. Plus they are like an advertising sign, inviting negative energies and entities to come and bother you or worse. ***Sound, clear psychic power requires a peaceful spirit, heart and mind.***

How To Purge Negativity

1. Take the stance that you will not allow negative energy to reside within your heart, mind or spirit. Be vigorous in not speaking negatively yourself and purging negativity when you realize it is festering inside of you.
2. If a negative thought or emotion wells up, allow yourself to vent it out. If you are mad at yourself, someone else, or a situation, don't just push it down and try to forget about it. Look at the wall and imagine you are speaking to the person or the situation, or yourself. Don't hold back your words or emotions and tell them why you are upset.
3. It is absolutely not necessary in most cases to confront

the person or situation, unless there is an issue that can only be resolved by talking directly. In most cases, confrontation will only lead to additional anger and upset. Purging your anger, hurt, loss and upset to the impassive wall is very therapeutic and usually more than adequate.

4. After the wall purge go outside and find a rock that will fit inside your curled hand. Hold the rock in your hand and looking at it say, "Rock, into you I send all of my (anger, upset, hurt feelings, etc.)" Then throw it far from you and shout "Begone!" And so it shall be. If negativity return about something else, simply repeat the procedure until it is gone forever.

A Banishing Spell/Prayer

Some people are afraid to use any type of spell or incantation, but you shouldn't be as long as it is for a purpose of light. In fact, I find spells to be like focused prayers. To create a spell that rhymes and makes sense requires some thought and effort. Here's one you can use or modify that incorporates getting rid of your garbage utilizing a rock. *Concisely fill in the blank with as few words as possible describing the particular trash issue. Such as "dark energy of my work", or dark energy of my relationship with_____", or "dark energy of my memory of _____."*

Dark energy of _____ lurking about like a disease

begone forever, bring no more unease.

The essence of feeling, which aches in my heart as if stabbed by a thorn,

(or The essence of thought, which aches in my head as if stabbed by a thorn,)

I forever cast away sealed within this rock, which none shall mourn.

This I command, this I decree,

Now and forever, so let it be.

Chapter 9

PSYCHIC OVERLOAD

As you use your psychic abilities more and more, it is like finding yourself on a new planet where everything is different from what you have known and are accustomed to in your life. There are a great many fresh sensations and new situations that you must ponder to understand. Of course you're anxious and insatiable to learn and experience more and more. It's exciting, It's fulfilling. It's wonderful! But it can also knock you down suddenly and drain all of your energy if you take in and experience too much too fast. Just like any muscle, you need to strengthen your psychic abilities by regular and ever increasing use, while also being wise not to overdo it.

This is true not just for the novice, but even for very practiced and experienced individuals. All of us can experience a total fatigue of our physical body and mental and emotional well-being if we take on too much psychic exercise in too short of a time. The more psychically adept you become, the more psychic input you will begin to receive unbidden from many sources. Just like you have learned to tune out many of the sensory inputs received by your physical senses so you are not overwhelmed by everything you see, hear, and smell, you also have to acquire the ability to filter out psychic input that you have not sought. This is especially true while you are consciously aware and awake.

Think of yourself as a bottle. Every psychic input you receive pours psychic energy into your bottle. The more you get, the bigger your bottle becomes. That's great, it shows you are growing. But if too much psychic energy pours into you faster than your bottle can grow, the psychic energy spills out causing you to have psychic overload.

Psychic overload is easy to defend against. It's not like it's a poltergeist trying to harm you. At the beginning of your day, or during the day if you suddenly seem to be getting a lot of unsolicited psychic energy, simply create a Mirror ASP close to your body to reflect any undesired psychic energy back to where it came from.

Don't let the ease of dealing with this challenge lessen its importance. Insuring you are never psychically overloaded, keeps your physical body energetic, your emotional level grounded, your mental abilities clear and most importantly leaves you plenty of room in your psychic bottle to receive and work with the psychic energies that you choose.

Chapter 10

EMPATHETIC OVERLOAD

Some psychics cultivate the gift of psychic empathy. Through conscious or subconscious interaction of their auric field with other peoples, and a desire and focus to understand their emotions, Empaths are able to feel in their heart, exactly what is being felt in the heart of the person they are tuning into.

If the person is happy or euphoric, then it's a natural high for the Empath as well. But if the person is traumatized, fearful, despairing, or experiencing any negative emotion, their feeling will also weigh heavily on the Empath as it sinks into their own heart.

In this case, you cannot use a Mirror ASP, because that would be counterproductive to being open and receptive of another persons feelings. However, an Absorb ASP is very useful for Empaths. The Absorb ASP will take in the emotional energy radiating from the other person. Because the ASP is within the space of the Empath's aura, they will be able to sense the emotions caught up in the shield, if they choose. They will still thoroughly know the feelings of the other person, while safely being shielded from having any negative energy entering into their own inner core.

PSYCHIC SELF DEFENSE

Chapter 11

DISMISSIVE OPINIONS

Have you ever been feeling great, happy about what you are doing or is happening in your life, excited to share what's exciting you with friends and family, only to have them shoot down your high flying balloon with negative comments and derisive opinions? Thus is the life of the psychic and paranormal practitioner living in a world of mundane people who do not understand anything about you, and are usually afraid of what they don't understand. Classic Harry Potter and the Muggles, only this is real life.

Even well intentioned and loving family members can dampen your enthusiasm and make you question your actions. Because they are your family and you love them and they love you, any negative comments, or caustic or even mild unsolicited negative opinions they give about your psychic explorations, carry more weight than those of other people.

This type of negative energy can be quite disruptive and greatly inhibit your ability to utilize your psychic powers. At the least, they sour your mood and make you unable to connect to your psychic source. At worst, they can completely derail you and make you wonder if you just want to get off the psychic train at the next station for good.

Luckily this is another easy challenge to solve. You simply need to decide if a Mirror ASP or an Absorb ASP would be most appropriate. If you are dealing with family or close friends, an Absorb ASP would be most appropriate. Negative energy they willingly or unknowingly hurl at you will simply be absorbed by the shield. It will not affect you in any way. You'll be able to honor their opinion, without having your own mood or thoughts changed in the least. Nor will there be any consequences for them. You love them and don't want them to feel bad either. With an Absorb ASP, they will not. You two will simply be having a conversation with differing opinions without either swaying the others opinion, but also without either being hurt in any way.

If you are dealing with people who you feel are maliciously trying to hurt you by the negative comments they are making, especially if they are making their comments around other people trying to embarrass you, a Mirror ASP is more appropriate. It will bounce back the negative energy they were sending you right back upon them. The shoes they were hoping to make you wear they will find on their own feet instead. If you are in a group of people, the person making negative comments at you will instead find the others upset or making fun of them for their comments.

Chapter 12

NEGATIVE ENERGY PEOPLE

Occasionally you will run into nice people, who despite saying or doing nothing of a disharmonious nature, still drain you of energy and affect your mood negatively. Often times they know they have that affect on people and they feel hopeless. They want friends, they want acceptance, they have no desire to hurt anyone, they want to be part of the group, but they realize something undefinable about them drives people away.

When you encounter people like this, in good conscience you should not abandon them and simply run away as everyone else has done. First protect yourself with an Absorb ASP, then, if they know they have a problem and are willing to accept help, offer to use your gifts to help them. It will be a great blessing and they will be forever grateful.

The root of problems like this, though they may stem from a variety of life incidents, ultimately are reflected in a very out-of-balance auric field. The first step will have a huge and immediate affect. Simply instruct the person how to ground and balance their 7 major energy centers. It works for you too!

To Ground:
1. Stand outside with your bare feet on green grass. If it is

winter and the ground is too cold or covered with snow, stand indoors on a natural wood or stone floor, on the lowest level of a home or building.

2. Tilt your head back and raise your face to the sky. Lift your arms up high above your head with palms facing up.

3. Envision a beam of energy flowing from the universe through you, down into the ground.

4. Grab hold of the beam of energy and pull it slowly down through your body with your hands and bending over push it through your legs, out your feet and deep into the earth.

5. Visualize the energy beam now coming from the center of the earth running through your body from your feet, swirling all around inside of you, then looping back into the earth. You are now firmly grounded in an Earth Loop. You are also still connected to the universal energies in the heavens above, should you wish to call upon them.

6. Repeat 2-3 more times if needed. When you have succeeded you will feel calm, peaceful, grounded and not easily disturbed.

In the traditional eastern philosophy the energy centers are called "chakras." I use the Celestine Light energy system for greater accuracy. In Celestine Light the energy centers are called "Root Ki."

To Balance the Energy Centers:

Find a comfortable place to sit. If you are relaxed sitting on the ground in the traditional cross-legged position you may do so. But sitting in a chair with your feet on the floor is fine as well. Join your hands together in the prayer position right in front of your chest.

Now visualize the Root Ki energy centers. They are not monotone in color. The color is most intense toward the center and lightens and diffuses as it expands outward. The colors resonate with the energy of the Root Ki and also have a harmonic resonance with specific musical notes and sound frequencies expressed in hertz.

The first is called **Xe**; spelled XE. This is the center of your

Negative Energy People

psychic abilities. It is purple in color and resides just above your head. It corresponds to the musical note of F*b* and the frequency of 678.41.

The second is the **Ka**; spelled KA. It is the energy center of your mind and thoughts, both conscious and sub-conscious. It is centered around your head and is a dark blue color. It corresponds to the musical note of D and the frequency of 588.86.

The third is the **Qo**; spelled QO. It is the energy nexus for your self-confidence, self-expression and self-esteem. It is turquoise in color and located just below your chin around the area of your

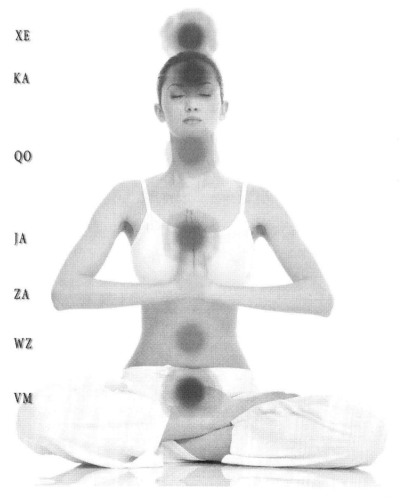

neck. It corresponds to the musical note of D♭ and the frequency of 566.03.

The fourth is called **Ja**; spelled JA. This is your heart center, the well of your emotions, and is centered around your chest. It is green in color. It corresponds to the musical note of C and the frequency of 527.35.

The fifth is the **Za**; spelled ZA. This is the location for primal instincts as well as past life memories. It is yellow in color and is centered around your diaphragm. It corresponds to the musical note of B♭ and the frequency of 472.27.

The sixth is the **Wz**; spelled WZ. This is the center for energy associated with your physical health and physical body. It is located near the navel and a bit above. It has an orange color and corresponds to the musical note of A and the frequency of 440.

The seventh is the **Vm**; spelled VM. This is the center for sexuality, reproduction, and creativity. See it as red in color and located just below the abdominal area and slightly above the groin area. It corresponds to the musical note of G♭ and the frequency of 757.53.

In the following order visualize an omnidirectional, swirling sphere of energy at each location. Visualize one energy center at a time and go through this visualization for each one.

a. See the energy sphere spinning omni-directionally.

b. Visualize it slowing down

c. Visualize it speeding up

d. Visualize it expanding beyond your body.

e. Visualize it contracting down to a sphere the size of a tennis ball

f. Visualize it returning to normal size, a little smaller than the width of the body at the spot it is located.

g. Visualize it returning to a normal omnidirectional spin and speed.

h. Proceed to the next energy center and repeat.

Chapter 13

ENERGY DAMPENING LOCATIONS

Certain physical locations are full of negative energy. For reasons that may remain unknown to you, they will dampen your energy and mood very quickly when you are at one of these locations. Some of the sources of the problem include: electromagnetic radiation from overhead power lines, excessive gravitational fields from iron concentration in the earth, site of death, especially massive death such as battlefields and the location of a negative energy vortex.

In a home or building you can also experience Energy Dampening spots. The structure may have been built over a burial ground, battleground, or some other negative event that occurred in the past. Electromagnetic sources from computers to many modern appliances are also common sources of negative disruptions of your energy inside a building.

Certain locations, normally very specific spots, also can have high concentrations of naturally occurring psychic energy that a sensitive person will pick up on right away. But non-sensitive people will be affected as well. These locations are more often positive energy spots rather than negative. But the dampening effect might still be felt because the energy at these locations is so strong and concentrated, it simply overloads you. It can discombobulate your thoughts and emotions, as well as your physical balance for reasons that will seem perplexing unless you identify what is causing the psychic concentration.

If it is a positive energy it will usually be from a natural source source such as a concentration of quartz crystals or other energetic minerals, or from a Positive Energy Vortex. I have been to numerous positive vortexes, including the well known ones in Sedona, Arizona and the more numerous and powerful ones in Northern California and Southern Oregon. Some of the latter emit such intense energy fields that it is sometimes difficult to stand up without swaying with the movement of the energy and losing your balance.

At locations such as Stonehenge, and other unique or sacred sites created by man, you can also experience psychic energy concentrations of sufficient intensity to disrupt you. The geometric shape of structures is often a major contributor, if not sole reason, it is able to act as a psychic energy concentrator. Some locations have positive energy and others concentrate and emit negative energy.

If you are in a known area of concentrated psychic energy, you will know after your first visit whether you can handle it or not. If you do not have any discombobulation, loss of balance, queasy stomach, dry lips, sudden overly emotional reactions, or other typical manifestations, then you should just enjoy the extra energy and test some of your abilities, which should be enhanced at any of the positive localities.

If the location emits a strong negative energy, even if you feel you are not affected, it would be wise to protect yourself with either a Mirror or Absorb ASP, whichever you feel would be most effective. When you are surrounded by negative energy, regardless of its source, it does wear on you until it wears you down. It is always a good idea to protect yourself and neutralize the threat. Even a mighty, towering oak can be felled by nonstop chipping at its trunk.

Chapter 14:

CLEANSING A HOME OF NEGATIVE ENERGY

As humans, we are innately very sensitive to unseen energies, both the uplifting and the depressing, the inspiring and the malevolent. Much more than is credited, our sensitivity often has to do with very subtle body language and almost imperceptible micro facial expressions. Simply looking at someone's face, even when no words are spoken or movements made, can tell you a whole story about their mood at the moment. Most people subconsciously perceive other peoples moods because the subtleties of their eyes and face are shouting it out, even while they may be silent. But beyond what you intuitively understand from subtle body language, your are also sensitive to pure emotional energy that remains behind, often for a very long time, after the originating person has departed.

If you want to try a quick cool experiment, go put on a jacket another person you know frequently wears. When you first put it on, if you are aware of energy at all, you will momentarily feel as if you are that person, because their energy is so imbued in the clothing that often surrounds their body.

- Have you ever wandered into a room and been happily welcomed by a friend, but left with a nagging feeling that something was amiss and that their upbeat persona was a facade?
- Have you ever entered a room with two or more people

that cheerily greet you with smiles, but you are left with an unsettled feeling that they have just been arguing?

- Have you ever walked into a vacant room, a home, an office or a building, and almost had the hairs on the nape of your neck stand up as you immediately had a foreboding sense of danger?

- Have you ever been walking out in the forest or an open meadow and suddenly had an inexplicable feeling of sadness come over you?

In any location, when something as simple as a heated argument erupts, it leaves an unseen negative energy residue behind that will affect anyone that comes within its field, until the energy has dissipated. If it was a minor argument the energy may disappear in a matter of hours. A more heated argument may take days to clear out through natural dissipation.

Even when no argument occurred, negative energy can still accumulate. Maybe you came home after a hard day at work, just feeling blah and went through the rest of the day in a lethargic foul mood. Every time that occurs you make a negative energy deposit in your home. No big deal if it's only one day, but come home like that several days and you will be building up a reservoir of negative energy in your home that will continue to detrimentally affect you and any visitors until you clear it.

Or perhaps you had a friend come over who just wants a non-judgmental buddy to empathize with his depression and listen to his woes about a recent breakup with his girlfriend. He may go home cheered up and happy he came to talk to you, but he left a residue of negative emotional energy behind.

The more serious problems arise when a location was the scene of not just one argument, but a series of heated disagreements that continued to take place in the same home or room over a period of time. In these cases, the negative energy never has time to dissipate, and instead begins to accrue stronger and stronger with each additional negative emotional energy disruption.

When you enter a space either outside or in a building that is

Cleansing a Home of Negative Energy

holding negative emotional energy, if you spend any time in that spot you will be affected by the energy. The most common indicator that something is amiss is when you become increasingly negative yourself, out of the blue and for no apparent reason whatsoever. You may have been in a perfectly happy and optimistic mood before you arrived. But after only a short time in the room or building or upon the land, you may find yourself becoming more negative or critical in your thoughts and increasingly judgmental of other people, even those that aren't present, but that you are only thinking about! If there is another person present, you may find you quickly and unreasonably go from calm to anger in your words or actions toward them, instigated by trivial perceived slights. Your emotional reactions become far disproportionate to the conversation or situation. Even while in the midst of your unreasonable emotional outburst, you will often realize you are out-of-line to be acting and speaking the way you are, thinking to yourself, 'this isn't me', and wondering why you are behaving like you just ate some locoweed.

When these situations occur most people think the problem is with them. They will apologize and try to make up for their idiotic actions and words. But if their actions seem out of character, than the root of the problem is not likely them at all, but the lingering negative emotional energy in the room, building, or upon the land, that energetically prodded them into their hurtful actions or words. Rather than dissipating the negative energy residing, their own harsh words or actions have augmented it, making it more likely similar situations will continue to arise in that location!

Of course there are degrees of negative energy, both in the power of the initial energy and the length of time it will linger. A small argument that occurred in a room is inconsequential. The negative energy will dissipate within an hour or two. Even if you wandered into the room while it still hung heavy with the recent negativity, its power is so small and insignificant you are not likely tot be affected.

Sometimes however, horrendous events occurred in a room or a home, such as violent assault, forcible rape, murder or even a massacre that took many lives. It does not need to be a person on person incident either. Perhaps someone drowned or was killed in an accident at that location. In these more serious incidents, the negative emotional energy is potent and detrimental. It will linger for years, negatively affecting every person that ever spends any time in that space. In particularly abhorrent incidents it can remain as a malevolent energy for decades and even centuries. Compounding the situation, other dark energies, entities, and malignant beings are drawn to such wells of melancholy. Their presence makes a bad situation worse. *If you suspect that in addition to negative emotional energy lingering in a location, there might also be dark entities of any type also present, please refer to the chapters on those beings for the specific methods necessary to banish them.*

Whenever you are moving into a home that other people have previously lived in, or renting a commercial space where other businesses once were, or even building a new home on a piece of property where indigenous people might once have dwelt, you would be wise to first clear the space of any lingering negative energy. The older the home or building is, the more people have occupied it, the more likely that is has been the scene of numerous outpourings of negative emotional energy from heated arguments or worse. Simple counter measures can nullify and dissipate any and all intensities of negative emotional energy, allowing you to confidently move into a pristine energy location, despite what may have occurred before your arrival.

Straightening Up

In any occupied home the first step of dispelling negative energy should be straightening the place up. When someone is in a negative space, they often become slovenly, leaving clothes on the floor, food crumbs scattered about, unwashed dishes piled in the sink, beds unmade, pillows askew on the chairs and couches, bathroom counters and sinks covered with scum and toothpaste, and the floors full of junk from neglecting vacuuming. Cleaning house and putting everything in order is an important preliminary step to vanquishing the negative energy. A lot of negative energy can actually be residing in that mess! If your home is in so great a disarray that just the thought of having to clean it is overwhelming and depressing, call on some family and friends to help out, or even hire a cleaning service to come in on a one time basis to do it for you. But don't neglect this important step.

Burning Sage

A common method used by many psychic practitioners to energetically purify a space is to burn a hand-held bundle of the herb White Sage, which can be picked up at most metaphysical stores. This is commonly known as 'smudging.' Walking around the premises so the smoke thoroughly permeates every area, the doorways and the furniture, is reputed to be effective for ridding both lingering negative emotional energy as well as simple negative entities. Large bird feathers like from a hawk, are commonly used to push the smoke into every nook and cranny. Thoroughness is considered to be essential to effectiveness. Wafting the smoke on your face and body is also believed by many to clear your own aura of negativity. This method is used extensively by many Native Americans in their ceremonies.

Smudging is certainly helpful if it is done thoroughly. Some people have have reported less than satisfactory results. A little investigations finds that it was most often from lack of thoroughness. They did not realize the importance of this aspect, and simply let the sage burn in a single spot in the room, or haphazardly roamed about the room smudging.

However, some people like me, cannot tolerate any type of smoke. I even bring sandwiches when I go camping because I will not build a campfire. I've met other people who are allergic to sage in a smoke form. It actually causes puffy eyes, runny nose and skin irritation. An effective alternative is to use sage essential oil, diluted in water 10-30 drops to a pint, and then spray it as a mist through an atomizer. Atomizers are the spray nozzles like those found on perfume bottles that produces an exceptionally fine mist. The mist lingers longer and in my experience is even more effective than the sage smoke. The key still being thoroughness of application. People who are allergic to the smoke seem to not be bothered by the atomized spray.

Salt

The use of salt for both purifying and banishing dark energy and entities is an ancient ritual. Its effectiveness is attested to in texts of both white and dark magic. Any pure salt without additives can be used. I have had exceptionally good results using the pink Himalayan salt, which contains numerous trace minerals. Plus, pink is a very calming and peaceful color and it strongly emits that energy throughout room.

Simply place a small pile of salt in the corner of each room you wish to clear. If it is a bedroom, also place a small pile of salt at the base of each leg of the bed. A thin line of a few grains of salt should also be spread along the base of all the walls and on top of the molding above every door.

If you are dealing with a particularly loathsome location that just exudes negative energy, you should take an extra step of using a well rung sponge mop to wash down all the walls with a mild salt water solution. Don't make it too strong or you will leave a salt residue on the walls. But even a greatly diluted solution is effective when it is spread over the entire area of the walls.

Prayer

Prayer is a potent force of brilliant white light. The good news is it does not matter which spiritual path or religion you adhere to, or which higher being you pray to, as long as your god or guide is conceived as a being of light. Whether your higher being of light is Jehovah, Great Spirit, Heavenly Mother, an angel, Allah, Gaea, Jesus, Ra, or any other, is unimportant.

The bad news is if you have no religion, if you believe there are no higher beings in the universe with your well-being in their

Cleansing a Home of Negative Energy

heart, you will be missing out on one of the most helpful steps in complete removal of negative emotional energy and lower level negative entities: prayer.

Your belief in higher beings of light and love that desire the best for you is a significant power that connects you to the greater energies of light in the universe, calling them to come and aid you in your life. It does not even matter if you are correct in your specific belief. It is the intent and the depth of your sincere belief that activates the positive energy. If you pray to Allah, but it's really Jehovah, or you pray to Heavenly Mother, but it's really Gaea, or you pray to Jesus, but it's really Ra, is literally inconsequential.

To utilize prayer for removal of negative emotional energy and simple negative entities, simply speak to the higher being of your belief, as you are going about your expunging negative energy rituals. Here are a few examples. Use your own words as appropriate for your situation.

- As you spray atomized sage throughout the room: "_____, I call upon you to purge this place of all negative emotional energy and negative entities."

- As you sprinkle a thin line of salt above each door way on top of the molding: _____, please make this room a sanctuary, that no negativity can enter and any currently here is expelled."

- As you clear land that may have had battles or death upon it: _____, I call upon you to bring your peace to this land. Refresh it with your positive white light and energy. Purge the energies of hate and anger. Call any spirits or entities that linger here to a place of greater light and peace."

Symbols

Symbols are powerful energy! If you have a religious or non-religious symbol that speaks to your heart and mind as an emblem of positive light and power, or a ward against negativity or negative entities, you can place that symbol around your home to keep out the dark and welcome in the light. Dip your finger in pure olive oil and lightly draw the symbol with the oil next to every door or window. You can also take a visible image of the symbol and place it somewhere in the room where you will see it. Every time you gaze upon it, positive light will come to you and energize you.

Music

The last step to totally refresh the energy in any location is to play it a joyful melody. You can choose to be present or away, but should let the music play continuously even if on a loop, for at least 3 hours. Any type of very upbeat, happy music (no singing), will be effective. Upbeat jazz or classical compositions such as Pachelbel Canon are great!

PART III
MEDIUM RISK THREATS

Chapter 15

ENTITIES & BLOBS

There's quite a numerous assortment of lower energy level entities that abound around us often referred to as 'entities' and 'blobs.' The terms are generally used synonymously, with entities sometimes given the nod as being as having a bit of consciousness, while the blobs just act instinctively without thought. Various religions have belief systems to account for them. They are not disembodied spirits. They have never had a body and do not have enough Soul Essence energy to exist in the body of even a primitive animal. Some are nothing more than vague, indistinct blobs of very faint negative energy. You can read a detailed description of these interesting energy creatures in the Oracles of Celestine Light: Vivus , chapters 94-98.

They cannot actively hurt you, but they are a drain on your energy and can end up causing you to hurt yourself or others. If you get enough of them attached to your auric field it can disrupt your energy sufficiently to have consequences. A little infestation will cause you to have a bad mood and be short tempered for no reason. A larger infestation may cause you to have a bout of depression and make bad choices regarding your own body, such as drug or alcohol use. A still larger infestation can cause your brain to disengage from rational thought and you can end up doing some really crazy things from having a sex orgy with strangers, to walking naked through town, to taking outrageous actions at work that get you fired.

A good deal of mental illness stems from an infestation of entities. Certainly removal of the entities by someone adept in

Psychic Self Defense

that ability can be extremely helpful.

The best defense is simply to avoid situations and locations where entities and blobs are typically found as much as is possible. Entities like dark places, but not completely dark. Any places where people have woes, or are witnessing other people with woes is a likely hot spot. Mental hospitals, taverns, horror shows at movie theaters, regular hospitals, graveyards, anywhere human suffering is depicted or taking place, you'll find entities.

If you must visit or work in one of the places like these, a Mirror ASP is essential. If you are going to be watching a movie or even a TV show with a lot of violence or dark themes, protect yourself with a Mirror ASP and drink 1/2 cup of salt water prior to viewing the show. Avoidance is even better.

Salt Water

As explained further below in the description of Disembodied Spirits, salt is an athema to them. It is like mosquito repellant for ghosts, entities and demons. Drinking a ½ cup of salt water is a quick way to rid your body of any other-wordly infestations, and to prevent any new ones while you are watching a dark

show or visiting a location where you might encounter the beasties. However, do not drink more than ½ cup as you can get sick from drinking salt water. And the effects of ½ cup will usually only last for about 2 hours of protection.

Chapter 16

SCENES OF DEATH & DESTRUCTION

If you have any type of psychic vision such as clairvoyance or precognition, you may sometimes see horrific scenes of misery, death and destruction. Once you are adept with these psychic gifts your visions will be exceptionally vivid. It will almost seem as if you are living within the scene. Obviously, living through hell on a regular basis can end up haunting your conscious thoughts. Both your everyday life and your psychic time can be seriously impeded if you cannot get horrible images and memories out of your mind.

I had this problem for years with one incident. Whenever something came up that reminded me of the serial killer Ted Bundy murdering my friend Georgeann,

Negative Energy Converter

the scenes of her abduction that I had witnessed a couple of years before in a precognitive dream, would keep replaying over and over in my mind. My work days would become very unproductive and my sleep elusive as I couldn't get those awful images out of my mind. Mentally, I understood that it was ridiculous to still be enmeshed in emotional feelings about an event that happened in 1974, with the murderer executed for his crimes in 1989, and that I had no way of knowing would actually occur when I had the precognitive vision. There was never a problem 99.9% of the time when I didn't think about the events. But when something would come up to remind me…I would end up with a discombobulated day and night.

I tried numerous methods to avoid the haunting thoughts whenever they returned, but to no avail. Finally, after seeing it in a vision, I found something that worked wonderful for me. I had to search a bit to find the components, but the combination of a sizable piece of turquoise with a black tourmaline crystal was amazingly effective at negating any discombobulating thoughts or emotional connection to the events. The memories were still there, they just no longer affected me. I ended up calling the Black tourmaline/turquoise combination a *Negative Energy Converter*.

The black tourmaline absorbs the negative energy of the memory and the blue turquoise cultivates peaceful, calm feelings. This allows the memory to be recalled without inflicting mental or emotional disruption. All that was necessary to invoke this power was to hold or have nearby, the tourmaline and turquoise Negative Energy Converter.

Another method I have not personally tried, but have had very good reports about from others is to use EFT Tapping to negate the bad memories.

Chapter 17

REGRETFUL ENERGY VAMPIRES

A particularly unfortunate individual is a regretful Energy Vampire. They made a choice before they came into this life to increase their Soul Essence energy by stealing it from others rather than creating it by their own efforts toward personal growth and expansion. However, they do not remember this choice and are often depressed because they do not understand why they are they way they are, and why they cannot change their nature, even though they sometimes try. Like their cousins the predator Energy Vampires, they are invigorated by personal confrontation and misery in others. But unlike the predator vampires, they often realize their behavior is wrong and wish it could be otherwise, not realizing this is their self-inflicted curse.

Where other people seek harmonious and peaceful relations, Energy Vampires need confrontation, turmoil and upset. The negative energy produced in upsetting situations is something they thrive on, to the point that it feeds them energetically by taking Soul Essence energy from the person they are in confrontation with. Because their precious Soul Energy essence is being forcefully sucked out them, of course the victim feels completely drained energetically and emotionally, while most often also ending up mentally discombobulated from the confrontation.

Most regretful Energy Vampires have a conscience and

oftentimes feel a some sorrow for their angry actions. They will often try to make amends by later being very nice and sweet. They know it is counterproductive to good relations to have verbally and emotionally violent confrontations. Yet, despite their attempts to maintain life and relationships on an even keel, things always turn sour. As much as they might desire it to be otherwise, they have a primal need for confrontation and the energy it brings them.

Energy vampires are always a challenge to deal with. Because you are struggling with their base energy makeup, one they made by choice before they came into this life, to be the template of their life, you will not change them; no more than you would be able to change the fundamental nature of a vampire that fed on human blood. A blood vampire might feel bad about drinking human blood, they might even rob a blood bank as an alternative to sucking it out of their victims; but their fundamental design would still require them to drink blood. It is the same for Energy Vampires, except through confrontation and discord they suck energy from the Soul Essence of their victims.

Please let me reiterate and make that perfectly clear. You cannot change the nature of an Energy Vampire. It would be like trying to change the race of a person into a different one. Even if the Energy Vampire regrets the damage they may cause in confrontations, even if they swear they will never do it again, they sadly cannot help themselves. They will do it again. And like an addict, over time they will need to escalate the intensity of the confrontations, the mental, emotional and verbal abuse, in order to receive the needed level of energetic satisfaction.

Your best defense against any type of Energy Vampire is to cut them out of your life and avoid them entirely; no personal meetings, phone calls, texts or anything. Unfortunately, when you are dealing with family members, especially spouses or ex-spouses, total avoidance is not always possible.

If you must have meetings with an Energy Vampire, protect yourself with a powerful Mirror ASP. This will allow you to remain calm within the storm and not personally feed the confrontational fires. You still need to restrain yourself from responding. You can negate your own mirror shield if you choose to react and allow yourself to be drawn into a confrontation with the vampire. If you remain calm, the angry, negative energy hurled at you by the Energy Vampire will bounce back at them. A normal person would be stopped in their tracks by the bounce back; but the Energy Vampire will just feed on their own negative energy. It won't slow them down, but after a bit they usually become satiated, awash in their own energy and wind the confrontation down. If at any point in the confrontation you can physically get up and leave, you should do so; the earlier the better.

The only reason an regretful Energy Vampire is categorized as a medium risk rather than a high one, is that they do understand they are causing needless problems and with the best of intentions, they often make sincere efforts to limit or eliminate their confrontations. However, their confrontational nature will always return.

An Aura Note About Vampires

Energy Vampires are easy to identify before you have any need to interact with them once you are competent at viewing people's aura. The aura of a non-vampire will always flow with some harmony in its movement. Even if they are sick or upset, their aura will still move harmoniously, albeit with disruptions in the energy field over their areas of weakness. There will also be a distinct directional flow to the energy as it circulates through the the three pairs of Alpha-Omega Gateways in the body – the top of the head, soles of the feet, and palms of the hands. After seeing so many 'normal' auras it is startling to look at an Energy Vampire's aura because their auric energy field jerks erratically, and the flow of their energy through the Alpha-Omega Gateways is exactly opposite of all other people!

There Is No Cure, But There Is A Restraint

As mentioned clearly, you cannot change the basic nature of an Energy Vampire. But with the reluctant variety, those who are truly sorry for the disruption they cause in other peoples lives, you can restrain their dark side. This is only possible if they are willing and only should be considered if they are part of a relationship with another person where both parties truly want to continue the relationship for all the good aspects that remain.

1. It begins with pink. The color pink is a very potent neutralizer of vampire energy. Even if the vampire is a man, they should have as many pink items in their life as possible without going overboard. Pink underwear, pink walls in some rooms, pink bed clothes and pillows. Pink is important.
2. The next requirement may be even more challenging for some. They need to become vegetarians or at the very least pescatarians (vegetarians that also eat fish). This should be done prudently and gradually to insure it is built on a foundation of good nutrition and knowledgeable food preparation. It is not really practical for one person of a relationship to be a vegetarian and the other to not be. So this regime also requires the non-vampire member of the relationship to adopt the vegetarian lifestyle as well. You will find that not eating meat, which has the energy of death, fear, and agony in it, will be a tremendous boon to not having those energies in the aura of the vampire.
3. Thirdly, you need to eliminate playing of discordant music. There are many genres of music that have pleasant harmonies to the flow of the music. Any of them are fine. But discordant music such as acid rock, are a stimulus that bring out the vampire tendencies. Eliminate them and you eliminate potential occurrences of the vampire nature.
4. The final important change is to eliminate as much

as possible, shows and movies that depict violence and gore. The more violent and graphic it is the more likely it is to trigger vampire tendencies. The more these four life changes are instituted the more the natural vampire tendencies will be suppressed, even to the point of virtual elimination. If both parties in the relationship are willing to take these steps, it can become a loving and fulfilling relationship in all ways, nearly every moment.

PSYCHIC SELF DEFENSE

PART IV
HIGH RISK THREATS

Psychic Self Defense

Chapter 18

DISEMBODIED SPIRITS & HAUNTED BUILDINGS AND LOCALITIES

Ghosts, also known as disembodied spirits, are the coherent energy remnants of people that have died. They have left behind a cognizant quantity of their Soul Essence energy instead of taking it all with them into the next life. Sometimes, all of their Soul Essence energy may remain behind as they never moved on to the next life at all! Over time the ghostly energy remnant will fade and eventually disappear completely. Without a physical body to contain it, the Soul Essence energy cannot remain forever on the physical plane; it is inexorably drawn to a realm beyond. But if it was a strong deposit of energy to begin with, the dissipation can take hundreds of years unless the ghost resolves their issues or realizes it is fruitless to cling to what they can never again have.

Most importantly as it relates to interactions with living people, is that disembodied spirits still have use of their mind and memory. The degree of mental clarity will vary depending upon the strength of their remnant energy that remained behind. This enables them to make conscious choices and actions, unlike mostly mindless entities and completely mindless blobs that are merely parasitically drawn to a person's energy.

Usually disembodied spirits are physically tied to a specific location by the energy of that spot that resonates enough with them to allow them to remain. If something tragic occurred to them and they haven't released the pain, they will still be able to maintain their energy at that location. If they had an obsessive fixation on a house or place, such as their own home, their energy can remain behind and manifest itself in various ways, until they no longer cling to that which is beyond their reach. If they had a very great love for someone, their energy can remain and they can manifest their energy in the rooms they most frequented together with their love.

With haunted houses or locations there may be an assortment of disembodied beings present from simple blobs, to slightly conscious entities, to fully aware spirits of the deceased, to sophisticated demons. If a location is hospitable to one type, it will usually be infested with others as well.

Most disembodied spirits do not have malevolent intent. Many may have positive purposes and actually be aids in keeping out negative spirits and influences and useful to you in multiple ways. How you feel about a spirit, welcoming and curious, or anxious and uncertain, are your auras way of telling you whether they are good spirits to keep around, or bad spirits to be rid of.

By definition, a disembodied spirit (ghost) has no physical substance. Nevertheless, they can affect physical objects in direct correlation to how strong their auric energy is that remains and how practiced they are in using it. These movements are caused by exerting telekinetic force, and obviously not by physically touching objects. This was depicted well in the movie 'Ghost.'

A weak effort would be to move an object a slight, but noticeable distance out of place, such as removing a book from a bookcase and letting it fall directly below on the floor. A greater effort would be aiming the book for a specific person or target as it is propelled out of the bookcase. A malevolent spirit may try to psychically harm someone by dropping objects on their head or putting them in spots where the living person might trip and take a dangerous fall.

In addition to possible physical threats, if you are in a building haunted by a spirit, especially one manifesting the movement of physical objects or creating spooky, inexplicable sounds, you can become mentally and emotionally distressed. This in turn is likely to affect your ability to call upon and use your psychic gifts.

An Absorb ASP coupled with a Transform ASP is quite effective for dealing with the malevolent actions of most spirits. Any negative energy sent your way is absorbed into the shield. As it is a shield of light attached to your aura, as long as your aura is strong, the darkness in the energy is changed to light. This can become quiet frustrating for disembodied spirits as you are able to simply ignore and be unflustered by anything they do.

Exorcising A Building

Occasionally, if there is a really malevolent, powerful spirit involved, you may need to exorcise them from the building. This is not the same procedure as exorcising a person who is possessed by something evil. But the effect is the same - the spirit or spirits will be gone.

There are multiple methods, most based upon one religion or another, to exorcise spirits from homes and other buildings. If the spirit was a follower of a particular religion while they were alive, that religion's exorcism procedures will likely work to rid the building of the spirit. However, as it is unlikely that you will know which religion the spirit followed in life, religious based exorcisms only have sporadic success. The exception would be if you were in a country or neighborhood where nearly the entire population followed the same religion, such as all Jewish or all Catholic. Then it is far more likely the exorcism procedures of the religion matching the population would work.

A very ancient method that works 98% of the time and on spirits of all religious persuasions, including those with no religion, or those that worship evil, is to surround them with a barrier of natural salt leaving open one escape route. Threaten to forever close the escape route and you'll see a mad rush to get out of the house by every spirit in it; except for the 2% that are either too ornery, or too vacant in their mind to care.

Why salt works so well is open to debate. I believe that because pure salt is a natural substance of the Earth, it is very grounded to the planet. It exerts a powerful magnetic auric force upon spirits that are no longer of this world, binding them to the planet. Though they may have haunted a place for centuries, the thought of never being able to leave is incredibly frightening to them.

Salt also easily combines with other substances. It somehow interferes with the auric fields of all types of disembodied beings and energies from simple blobs, to entities, to ghosts to demons. Salt is a threat to their very existence. It is a powerful counter against them, and has been used for this purpose since the dawn of recorded history by many, many cultures.

The Procedure Is Thus:

1. Obtain several pounds of natural sea salt or pink Himalayan salt. The Himalayan salt seems to be effective 98% of the time and sea salt about 95%. Determine the exact area within a building that the spirit moves about. Sometimes this will be a single room. Other times several locations may be involved. If you are unsure or if the entire building is haunted, treat the whole building.

2. Pour an uninterrupted line of salt completely around the perimeter of the building or whatever room or rooms you have deduced need exorcism. As you are pouring speak out loud to the spirit or spirits. Tell them you are encircling them with salt and that once the circle is completed they will be forever bound to that building or room. Tell them you are going further and that every room will also have a bowl of salt in it, creating a permeating energy that will forever be heavy and burdensome, perhaps even caustic to them.

3. Tell them you mean them no harm and invite them to leave several times while you are spreading the salt. When you have completely encircled the area you

are exorcising except for a small strip the width of a doorway, tell them in a loud voice that this is their last chance. You are about to bind them forever to earth and forever to this exact spot on earth. They will never be free again.
4. Tell them they have 10 seconds to leave or condemn themselves to forever be bound. The choice is theirs. Immediately, begin a countdown 10, 9, 8, 7, … before you finish you will feel a rush of air as all the spirits in the exorcised location hastily flee before it is too late and they are forever bound in place. Even the blobs, which would have not understood a single word you spoke, will flee the aurically caustic encirclement of salt.
5. Technically, the salt perimeter will not work with every type of disembodied beastie, particularly demons. But most don't know whether it will or will not do what you are claiming - to bind them in place. The fact that salt is an irritant to them at least, and caustic at worst, lends credibility to your threat. It seems the fear of the possibility of being bound is enough to motivate virtually all of them to make a hasty and permanent exit.
6. If you are worried about future hauntings, leave the perimeter of salt in place with just the one open space the width of a door. Any spirits contemplating even visiting, will change their mind when they see it would only take a few seconds to bind them forever in place.
7. Though I gave this as a description for exorcising a room, house, or building of ghosts, it works equally well for all types of lower disembodied beasties such as blobs and entities. It will even work for some demons.

Chapter 19

ALIEN PRESENCE

I've never had a face-to-face alien encounter, but I know and have helped people that have. I have no doubt aliens from other worlds can and do visit our planet. On multiple occasions on trips far into the wilderness, away from all city lights and all trappings of man, I have seen the lights of UFO's close up, flying in places no flying ships or lights should or could be.

In 1999, observations with the Hubble Space Telescope led to a conservative estimate that there were at least 125 billion galaxies in the universe. Scientists further estimate that there are at least 10 trillion planets just in our own mid-size Milky Way galaxy. Multiplying it out, 10 trillion planets x 125 billion galaxies, is a very, very, very, big number of potential worlds full of life.

Just from a logical standpoint, it is the height of ego gone wild to assert that in a universe of billions of galaxies, each containing trillions of planets, that our Earth is the only one with intelligent life. Can anyone really make that assertion with a straight face? Just within our own galaxy the Earth is nothing more than a tiny spec of dust in relation to the size of the galaxy. Then our galaxy is nothing but a tiny spec of dust in relation to the size of the universe. Is there anyone that honestly believes that our tiny speck of dust residing within another tiny speck of dust, is the only place in the unlimited vastness of the universe with intelligent life?

Given that any reasonable person would agree that the universe is probably full of intelligent life, the next question is how do we stack up on the intelligence and civilization scale?

Carborundum used as an Alien Alert

Geologically, our planet Earth has been dated to have existed for about 4.5 billion years. Anthropologists have determined that modern humans have been running around on the planet for a mere 65,000 years. The universe itself is dated by astrophysicists to be about 14.5 billion years old. That means for 10 billion years before our planet earth was even born, other planets had the opportunity to form, be populated by intelligent life, and have billions of years of evolution to progress before modern humans were even waking up in caves. So yes, I believe in aliens from other planets and I'm sure there are many that are as far advanced beyond us as we are beyond chimpanzees.

I don't know what motivates aliens. By their very nature they are...alien, and at this point, unfathomable. But abductions, implants, and other intrusive actions blamed on alien visitors, have happened with sufficient detail, related by enough traumatized people, all who pass lie detector tests, to make me a believer.

I had one particular friend that was being terrorized at night by what she believed to be alien visitors. She would wake up startled in the middle of the night and see beings with alien faces and thin bodies standing next to her bed. Within a second or two of awakening they would vanish. Her great fear was what

Wolf in Sheep's Clothing, Human

would happen, or already had, when she didn't awaken.

She asked me for help. After inquiring to a higher, more knowledgeable source, I was told about a combination of minerals that made an effective alien alarm. The basic mineral is raw carborundum (Silicon carbide).

It occurs very rarely in nature as the mineral moissanite. Usually it is a man-made substance, typically ground into fine pieces to make grinding wheels, ceramics and other uninteresting commercial uses. But in its raw state, it is a brilliantly hued, multi-faced crystalline substance. It has a harmonious interaction with your auric field and a strong reaction to non-human auras. When the carborundum is at your bedside within your auric sphere, if anything with a non-human aura, from an alien to a demon, passes thru the outside edge of your auric field, which is about 3 feet from you while you are sleeping, you will immediately be awakened from the energy disruption. If you lay a clear quartz sphere or pyramid on top of the piece of carborundum, it will extend its effective warning range about 3 times the usual distance from your body.

Chapter 20

DEMONS

Are demons real or just a fanciful construct of various religions? If they are real, where do they come from? These are questions I am asked from time to time, especially by people who profess no religion and consider demons, like gods, to just be religious myths.

Having come face to face with demons and fought them head on, I can assure you they are real and nothing to be trifled with. They may be big or small, but their capabilities are large compared to any other type of disembodied being. Most are not visible to your physical eyes. They often have powerful telekinetic abilities, but their specialty is tormenting or injuring you more subtly. They may have the ability to throw you off a bridge, but they derive much more pleasure from driving you to the point of despair where you commit suicide and throw yourself off the bridge.

As to where they come from - I have my own beliefs about that, but decline to impose them upon you. Various religions have differing ways to deal with demons and in my experience they are all effective if the person using them has courage, knowledge and confidence in prevailing. The foundation of any successful method to fight demons is to remember they come from a place of darkness and darkness cannot exist in the light. If you fight with light, with that which is good, noble and honorable, many means are effective in vanquishing demonic adversaries.

Please don't confuse the word 'light.' Though visible light is a potent power, you can't just shine a bright light on a demon and expect them to do anything but laugh. I use the words light and darkness both literally and metaphorically, with darkness representing reprehensible evil and light representing purity of heart and nobility of purpose. 'Light' in the context of fighting demons, means a purity of purpose and methods, coupled with an unselfish love in your heart to protect yourself or others from demonic attack.

The Movie 'Exorcist' Spawns A Demon

In my 20's, I was in the US Coast Guard stationed on Governors Island, New York. Our island was at an incredible location. The Statue of Liberty was just offshore and the tip of Manhattan and all the wonders of the big city, were just a short 10 minute ferry ride away.

One night after midnight, while I was alone in my room, I received a frantic, fearful call from my roommate Dan. I had never heard Dan be frantic or fearful about anything. He was 6'4" and a fit, muscular 240 pounds. Nobody in their right mind messed with Dan. But on this call his fear was palpable.

> *"Can you...come...and get me?" Dan stammered weakly.*
> *"What's going on Dan? Where are you?" I asked.*
> *"Hurry, before it's too late." He pleaded in a panic-stricken voice.*
> *"Hurry where?" I spoke firmly, trying to get him to think and speak rationally.*
> *"Ferry terminal...New York side...aahh...." These were his last words spoken in pain and then the line went dead.*

I rushed down to the Governor's Island ferry and luckily caught the next ferry just as it was getting ready to pull away from shore. I was the only passenger. From the moment Dan had called in agony, terrible thoughts of what might have happened to him ran continuously through my mind. I was sure he must be injured, maybe shot or knifed in a mugging. He should have known better than to be out by himself so late at night in the city.

Demons

As soon as the ferry landed I hurried off and into the terminal. It was completely empty except for the lone figure of Dan sitting hunched over at the end of a bench in the corner. I went to him quickly, relieved to not see any blood pooling on the floor or on his clothes.

Dan was just starring down at the floor, not even looking up at me. "What's the matter buddy?" I asked.

He shook his head slowly in silence for at least a minute. Then with great effort he quietly muttered. "I went to see the Exorcist movie...something happened to me...I think...I'm going to die."

I had not seen the movie and could not comprehend how a movie could have shaken him so thoroughly to his core. The ferry I arrived on returned to Governor's Island and Dan and I sat in the terminal talking for the next 20 minutes waiting for it to return. I reminded him it was just a movie, that nothing was real. By the time the ferry returned, friendship and consoling seemed to have restored the normal, stoic Dan I knew.

After boarding the small ferry, we went up to the open top deck to be in the fresh air and hopefully further clear Dan's head. Just as the ferry moved away from the dock it let out a blaring loud blast from its horn, which was mounted within 10 feet of where we were standing. We were both leaning against the rail looking at the Statue of Liberty in the distance. When the horn blasted Dan completely lost all control of sanity. Immediately he put his leg over the railing and attempted to leap over the side into the icy East River. Before I could react he already had both feet over the railing and was screaming like a madman as he balanced momentarily on the railing and made ready to jump.

I knew I had to act immediately and forcefully if I was going to prevent his jump. I'm short compared to Dan, so I shot my left arm up and encircled his neck. It was the only part of his body I knew I would be able to get a firm enough grip and leverage to counter his weight. Pulling back with all my strength I flipped him back over the rail. He ended up on his back laying on the cold metal ferry deck. Luckily, we were the only ones on the boat at that late hour and our maniac actions were not visible to anyone in the Pilothouse.

He reached up and held both of my arms with his hands and looked at me with a piercing gaze. "Help me," is all he said and then his eyes rolled up and he lay back on the deck breathing heavy.

When he had first called, I worried he was injured from a mugging. After I saw him and verified he was physically uninjured, I thought perhaps he had food poisoning or some other sudden illness. But when he tried to leap over the side of the ferry, I knew something else had control of him. I was too inexperienced at that point in my life, to know what exactly the problem was; but I knew instinctively it was not of our physical world.

As Dan lay on the deck, his breathing still coming in raspy gasps, I enveloped him deeply in my aura, connecting to every fiber of his being. I knew what his inner core aura normally felt like. I wanted to verify that it was still intact and normal. It wasn't! His inner core aura was in agony. It was twisting and convoluted as if it was fighting against itself. All of his energy centers were very diminished in size and erratic in their spin. I distinctly felt the aura of another being inside of him. A dark, foreboding, malevolent aura unlike any I had ever experienced.

Prior to this, I'm not sure I even believed in 'possession.' But that was obviously what had somehow occurred and I became an instant firm believer. Deciding to act quickly and forcefully to counter the evil, I laid my right hand on Dan's chest as I knelt beside him. Holding my left hand up to the starry night sky I called out, "Come to me energy of might and light." Instantly, I felt a rush of amazing energy like adrenaline multiplied by ten. I could feel a whirlwind of incredible energy swirling inside of me, and could see my own aura suddenly luminescent with white light and tiny jewels of many colors. For just a few seconds I swirled my auric energy closer and tighter, concentrating it. Then with a mental command, I sent it shooting down my right arm, through my hand and into Dan's chest. There was a loud anguished scream, but it wasn't coming from Dan! He lay on the deck with his eyes closed and seemed calm and serene. Seconds later he opened his eyes and I could tell immediately by his weak smile and peaceful eyes, that my friend was back.

As the ferry docked and we disembarked to walk back to our barracks we were both in our own thoughts and walked in silent contemplation. Climbing the steps to our building, Dan stopped and grabbed my arm. "Thank you. I think you saved my life." He said humbly.

"I think I just exorcised my first demon." I responded.

"Yeah, you did." He confirmed. "Yeah you did."

How To Cope With Demons

Unless you are a very advanced practitioner of the psychic and paranormal, I highly advise you to seek out someone that is an advanced practitioner if you feel you or someone you care about is being threatened by a demon. Like physical people, some demons are smart and others dimwits. But all can hurt you physically more than any other type of disembodied creature and they all have a passionate desire to do so. Worse, they can subtly convince you to injure yourself, especially with destructive habits such as drugs and alcohol. They are masters at influencing your emotions, making you feel depths of despair, agony, fear, worthlessness and loathing that you never imagined.

Why do they do these heinous actions? Unlike you and me and the billions of other people in the world, they will probably never have a physical body or an evolved spiritual body. They resent every person who does have the joy of a body and the many unique wonders it can experience. They will do everything in their power to get people in physical bodies to degrade and debase the great gift they are denied.

How To Tell If A Person Is Demon Possessed Or Just Mentally Ill

When you look at the dark lives of people like Hitler and other mass murders, or criminals that commit particularly gruesome and despicable crimes, you have to wonder if they did this on their own because they are fundamentally a heartless, evil person, or if they were completely mentally ill, or if they acted while under the influence of a demon. Certainly no well-adjusted person would ever commit many of the terrible crimes that seem all too frequent in today's world.

HERE'S HOW YOU TELL:

Mentally Ill: While there are a wide variety of symptoms for mental illness, depending upon the root problem, a mentally ill person will exhibit periodic to frequent bouts of aberrational behavior. Warning signs can include: big mood swings; irrational statements; problems with memory; inexplicable fatigue, difficulty expressing themselves logically; paranoid fears; sudden apathy; radical changes in sleep or eating patterns; new phobias; unexplainable increase or decrease in sexual desire; and any kind of uncharacteristic, peculiar behavior.

Possessed by a Demon: Balanced, positive people, who go through life with optimism rather than pessimism, and do not allow themselves to be put in an incapacitated state by alcohol or drugs, are rarely ever bothered or affected by demons. Demons are empowered by the fears and weaknesses of humans. They feed on human misery in every form. The more unbalanced and off track a person is in their life, the more susceptible they are to a demonic attack.

A person possessed by a demon may exhibit some of the symptoms of mental illness. But while a mentally ill person is usually disconnected from fully understanding they are mentally ill, a demon possessed person will be crying out for help, clearly knowing something is wrong with them beyond their control and desperately hoping someone can and will help them.

They often feel and express to others that they feel something unseen is attacking them or trying to influence them. The influences are often noticeable, particularly religious changes such as no longer wanting to go to church, temple or mosque, pray, or have any contact with crucifixes and any other religious objects. Demons hate anything associated with light, nobility, morality, or the divine, regardless of the religion.

Demonic influence is particularly noticeable when New Age people who often own many quartz crystals and other mineral power stones, are affected. If someone like this suddenly has an aversion to crystals and stones of power, especially to the point that they remove them from their house, it is a clear indication of demonic possession, especially if there are other signs present.

Another big sign is negative voices speaking in the mind. These can be both self-criticism and critical comments about others. Often the dark whispers will encourage breaking off relationships with good friends and encouragement to befriend new unsavory people.

Sudden desires to debase oneself in any way are another common indication of demonic influence or possession. These can include: sudden sexual promiscuity or infidelity, especially with a quick succession of multiple partners; an unexplained onset of aimlessness; increased alcohol or drug use; cruelty to animals or children; and disregard for rules and requirements, including the lack of desire to continue to do school or professional work competently.

Demons love to terrorize people in any way they can. Your fear is their food, your self-inflicted wounds their joy.

A truly bad person: When someone commits heinous acts without exhibiting the symptoms of mental illness or demonic possession or influence, they can be established as simply a depraved, twisted person. Perhaps they can blame it on their difficult childhood development. But the end result is often a monster who will appear as a perfectly normal person, one that you might even consider as a friend. A friend with an evil twin lurking inside. Many serial killers fall into this category.

An Effective Counterattack Against Demons

The best counterattack is the same as it is with all forms of self-defense from karate to jujitsu: avoid situations and places where you might be attacked, so you never need to use your self-defense abilities.

If you feel that you or someone you know is under attack, as I mentioned before, don't hesitate to call for assistance. Anyone from your local priest to a well-known psychic, to experts that specialize in ghost and demon hunting, can help.

Any item you have belief in can be a jewel of power for you to ward off demons. If you are a Wiccan and believe a pentagram has power over demons, so it shall be. If you are a Christian and believe a silver crucifix will drive demons away, so it shall be. If you are Jewish and believe a mezuzah on your door will thwart demons, so it shall be. If you are a New Ager and believe in the power of crystals to overcome demons, so it shall be. The stronger your faith and belief in the tools that you have a love and harmony for, the more powerful those tools will be. Faith is the real power. There is no mightier power in all the universe than faith.

Whatever defensive jewel you believe in, you can amplify its power by adding the energy of one or more fellow believers to it. For instance, if a Catholic priest blesses a Catholic crucifix, especially if it is specifically to ward off demons, his faith will be added to your own, making the power emanating from the crucifix that much more potent. If a Wiccan calls a coven and all within the group bless whatever object is chosen as the jewel of power, it will embody the faith and power of all those who blessed it.

Vocally imbue your jewel with the power of your faith, by holding it between your two hands and saying, "Within this jewel I call upon all the forces of good and light to reside. May it be empowered to thwart and repel demons by my faith and light and the faith and light of all who bless it."

Once you have your jewel of power, simply wearing it will repel most demons and keep them from possessing or influencing you. However, they can still be in your home or building and can cause mischief or injury by their actions. If this is the case use the salt perimeter described earlier. But before dispensing, have all the salt blessed by people of like faith, so the power of their faith is added to your own, dramatically increasing the potency and effectiveness of the salt.

These methods should rid most demons. Occasionally you may encounter an obstinate one. If your own training and understanding is not succeeding, don't be embarrassed or hesitant to call upon outside expert assistance.

Chapter 21

BLACK MAGIC

There are two things you need to guard against with Black Magic: someone that is trying to use it to hurt you; or hurting yourself by dabbling in occult activities without knowledge of what you are doing.

What is Black Magic? If it is something you are doing, it can broadly be considered any occult activity that is not drawing you to righteous purposes that is of benefit to you or others, or one that intentionally injures or manipulates anyone. If what you are doing is causing you or anyone else to be fearful or hurt emotionally, spiritually, physically or mentally, it is not a worthy pursuit, be it magic or mundane.

If it is something someone else is doing, it comes into the Black Magic realm when the actions involve using incantations, curses and tools such as voodoo dolls, to coalesce unseen energies to manipulate you and cause you to act in a way they desire, or attack and hurt you physically, mentally, emotionally or spiritually.

Magic itself is neither black or white. It is the intention in how it is used, either for good, uplifting and expanding purposes, or for evil, negative and dampening purposes, that earn it the monicker black or white. Unfortunately, there are both physical people and unseen beings that have devoted themselves to using paranormal energies for purposes that manipulate, hurt or injure others.

If you are learning about how to use spells, incantations and potions to harness energies to further your own desires, be careful not to slip off the higher path in your efforts to achieve your goals. Even something as innocuous as a love spell, depending upon how it is crafted and worded, can often be construed as black magic. If it is used to manipulate a person into having affections for someone they would not otherwise have amorous feelings for, then it is not of the light. If it is used to enhance your own beauty or improve your own personality that you might be more noticed and appreciated when you are talking with the one you have affections for, then it is non-manipulative of others, and of the light.

Your own choices and actions when dealing with the paranormal can expose you to the malevolent machinations of both people and unseen beings with dark intents. Dabbling in occult activities with little or no knowledge of the world you are calling upon, or the risks you are taking, lends itself to mischief from the unseen world. Sometimes the mischief can lead to serious physical and psychological harm.

Ouija Board horror stories, for example, from the experiences of countless innocent and paranormally ignorant inquirers, are legion. Do an Internet search for the subject. When I did, Google came up with 45,600 results. Typically a group of friends or family, all with little or no experience with the paranormal, gather around a Ouiji Board and just start playing around with silly questions. Sooner or later someone starts making paranormal type queries and then things can begin to get weird, soon progress from weird to scary, then from scary to dangerous.

Here's a typical result reported by Heather: *Then, they asked, 'Could you possess us?' and it pointed to 'yes.' They asked, 'could we help you?' and it pointed to 'yes' again. Then, being the idiot he was, my dad jokingly took a crucifix and touched it to the Ouija Board. The second it touched, Jesus fell off of the crucifix at hands & feet. My dad got royally freaked out and they decided to burn the board. A big mistake I swear to you. The next day, our house caught fire. My dad had to put it out with his hands seven times!!! Ever since then...strange things have been happening, and still do.*

Contacting disembodied spirits, attempting magic spells, or trying to exert or call any paranormal power without clear knowledge of the subject, techniques and risks, is opening a door to some unpleasant experiences. It's like jumping into a complex lab experiment in the middle of a chemistry class, when you have never taken the class and have no idea what the chemicals are that are being used, or the dangers of mixing them incorrectly.

If an inexperienced person ever feels compelled by peer pressure or their own inner promptings to ignorantly dabble with the paranormal despite the potential risks, there is one simple thing that can be done to significantly lower the dangers. Before beginning, gather together with everyone else involved, hold hands in a circle and have one person speaking for all, say, *As we seek now to (whatever you are going to do), we call upon all the forces of good and light to be with us. We only allow higher beings who have our safety and well-being at heart or in mind, to be present. By the power of the light within us, we forbid any being that would harm us in any way from manifesting in any form or action.* While not 100% foolproof protection, if said with power and forceful intent that procedure and incantation will keep most beasties at bay. If you are of a religious nature and you also call upon the Gods of your belief for protection, you will enhance your security still further. Your faith in the divine of your belief reinforces your own command that bars entry to beings of darkness.

How To Protect Against Personal Attacks

Two of the more common ways that someone may try to hurt you with black magic is through either voodoo or a magical curse. Many people are of the opinion that if they don't believe in Voodoo, black magic or curses, that they will automatically be unaffected because of thier disbelief. I am not of that opinion. Your auric field can and is disturbed by a wide variety of energetic influences from things your five senses encounter, to things you eat, to exposure to harmful chemicals or electromagnetic energy, just to name a few of the common ones. Except in exceptionally rare circumstances, if you drink a glass of cyanide poison, you will be dead quite promptly regardless of your belief to the contrary. It is the same for negative and dark forces – they can hurt you, even if you naively believe they cannot.

This chapter has really been all about negative energies of wide variety that can dampen your personal auric field and ultimately physically, psychologically, spiritually or emotionally hurt you. Voodoo and magical curses can do so just as easily as any of the other psychic threats you may encounter, especially if you are being attacked by someone experienced in perverting paranormal energies for destructive purposes.

Once again, avoidance of situations that might end up being threatening should still be your first defense. Don't give anyone a reason to want to hurt you with voodoo or a black magic curse. Live your life as a good person, empathetic and caring of others, positive and hopeful in your outlook on life, and willing to lend a hand and be of service. Cultivate positive people as friends and limit or end your association with negative, critical people, especially those who have dark, fearful, spiteful, or self-destructive tendencies. Who you are and the way you think and act, choosing positive over negative and light over darkness, creates an auric field that repels negativity and a permeating energy that makes you invisible as a target of evil intentions. I hope you don't think I'm preaching here. I am in no way trying to tell you how to live your life. I am simply giving you good advice based on a lot of experience as to a defense that is very effective.

Chapter 22

WOLF IN SHEEP'S CLOTHING, CHANNELED

Channeling from the modern era, and spiritualism from earlier ones, have always been popular psychic endeavors. Whether it is contacting higher beings from worlds beyond Earth, or the spirits of deceased people, being able to make a connection and communicate with beings beyond our physical Earth is a powerful draw.

But great care needs to be taken when communicating in this manner. Whether you are just asking questions of a Ouija Board, or entering into a full-trance channel where a higher being takes over your body and speaks through your vocal cords, opening the door to other beings can be dangerous.

For full-body, full-trance Channelers, there is a physical danger if they have not taken actions to protect themselves. A being that can control your body, can cause it to eat or drink harmful substances, or act in ways you never would.

As full-body, full-trance Channelers are very rare, the hazard for most other channelers, both novice and experienced, is the possibility of receiving false information that was thought to be true. Acting on the false information can lead to ruin. For example, you may have been told to buy a certain stock as it was going to quickly double in value. After rushing to invest your savings, the stock instead collapses and you loose your financial stability. Or you might be told to take a marvelous health cure, only to discover that instead it further worsened your health.

Just because you think you are channeling a higher being doesn't mean that is actually the case. Certainly it is helpful before you begin to state aloud that "*I only call and allow higher beings, who have advice that will help me to grow and expand in the light, to come and speak to me or through me.*" But on its own, those words only work in direct proportion to the power of your own aura and the strength of your own convictions. In some cases, with strong negative beings, those words alone will not work for anyone.

A good example of how people can be deceived, is channeling the archangel Michael. Michael is a popular higher being to channel, and there are many people who genuinely do, as the archangel is not committed to communicating only through one person. But how do you know that it is really the archangel Michael communicating? You are on Earth, the being communicating is somewhere else, and you have no way to verify with your physical senses who they are. Perhaps you feel a psychic resonance. While that is often a good confirming indicator, it is also not foolproof.

The Trojan Horse of Deceit

One of the sneakiest ways that disembodied beings, as well as living people that do not have your best interest at heart trick you, is to hide a damning falsehood among a bunch of truth. They will impart several gems of wisdom that reiterates and reinforces what you already know or believe to be true because it resonates with you. Because you accept these teachings as true you let down your mental and psychic defenses. Into that gap they slide a great falsehood. One that can cause you physical, mental and emotional pain or injury. They then quickly close the sandwich by spouting off again several things that are known and accepted as true. You may hear 95% truth that may seem at times to be uplifting and enlightening. But the 5% that is false can be so damaging that accepting any of the teachings becomes risky and a price likely to become painful to pay.

The Test of Truth

There is one foolproof test of any information purported to be coming from higher beings, or even from what you may think is your higher self. It works equally well testing any living teachers, gurus, prophets, etc. It doesn't matter whether you are the person channeling, or the person listening to a channeler or spiritualist and receiving the information they are dispensing. Apply this simple test and you will *always* know, if the wisdom imparted is true or false. To pass the test all three of these keys must be met:

Harmonious - Needful – Progressive

Harmonious: *Any information imparted must be harmonious with knowledge you already have that you know to be true.* If for instance, you had a friend that had shown you through many actions that they cared for you and had your best interests at heart, but then were told in a channeling that this friend was actually out to hurt you; that information would be contrary to all the evidence you had experienced; and if followed, could destroy a very supportive and beneficial relationship.

Needful: *You must have a need to hear this information at this time.* It must be useful information to help you in the present. True higher beings do not waste your time telling you something that has no application in your life today.

Progressive: *The information imparted must be new information, not just restating or emphasizing things you already knew.* For example, you might be told to 'eat more fruits and vegetables.' That would pass the first test, it would be harmonious with a lot of information available that lets us know that eating more fruits and vegetables should be an important part of everyone's diet. If you are lacking in your consumption of fruit and vegetables it might also pass the 'needful' test. But it wouldn't pass the 'progressive' test. Telling someone they should eat more fruits and vegetables on it's own is likely not progressive. Most people are already aware they should eat more fruits and vegetables. However, if you were told to eat more of a particular fruit or vegetable, because it had specific nutritional qualities you lacked and needed, then it would pass the 'progressive' test as well. Keying in on a specific beneficial food is probably not something you would have known on your own.

Chapter 23

WOLF IN SHEEP'S CLOTHING, HUMAN

There are living people who have set themselves up as enlightened teachers and gurus, that can also give you false, misleading and hurtful advice; often designed to benefit them at your expense. Some of these are well known celebrities, psychics, healers, or movement leaders. The same simple test of truth works just as well for anything they tell you or advise.

Ask yourself, is what they say is:

Harmonious - **Needful** – **Progressive**

In our modern era, more and more people have become disillusioned with traditional religions and the mind controlling, life dictating regimes that many of them espouse. Today there seems to be far more people who consider themselves 'spiritual' but not 'religious.' But humans have an innate need to 'belong', to be a part of groups and communities of like-minded people.

Some sincere, well-meaning, 'spiritual' but not 'religious' seekers of truth, end up following a self-proclaimed "guru" or "enlightened master" at some point in their life, most often in their 20's when they are most idealistic. This is often not because of bedrock belief in the teachings, but because of an affinity for the community or lifestyle. This is not necessarily a bad choice, and with enlightened teachers, who can be found upon many different paths, it can be a good one. The difference begins with the teacher or guru. The students tend to enjoy true benefit when the teachers are intent on selflessly helping their adherents in every way to have more fulfilling lives. But that is not the case with every guru or spiritual teacher; perhaps not even with many of them. And the followers should be choosing a path that truly brings them daily joy and fulfillment. One in which they are not following because they feel it is something they 'must' do, but rather a choice that they 'want' to do, and that they look forward to doing with happiness and anticipation.

It is easy to get caught up in the positive energy of a supportive, spiritual group, to the point that warning signs that would normally be heeded, beginning with your own intuition, are overlooked. The sad reality is many modern 'enlightened' teachers and gurus and no different in their true natures and hidden agendas than the hierarchy and priesthoods of the traditional religions: money, power over the people, and elevation to the fame of high positions of authority.

With that in mind, here are some warning signs to be alert for when sizing up the validity of purported gurus or 'enlightened' teachers. Added to listening to your own intuition, you have within yourself a very reliable means to see through the mirages and cut to the chases of reality.

1. $$$ Money $$$

Reciprocation is an important energy for personal growth. Certainly, if you have received something of value, to give something of value in return is a positive energy to be encouraged. Yet, a warning sign for false teachers is their focus on money first before enlightenment; particularly when the focus is on you paying **a lot** of money to receive their special enlightenment.

Whenever I am trying to decide if a purchase of any kind is 'worth it', I imagine two boxes; a '**Cost**' box and a '**Value**' box. Whichever box ends up being larger in the end is the choice I choose. The size of the cost box increases as I imagine throwing into it all of the cost associated with the proposed action. For instance, if I was considering going to a one day seminar by a well-known spiritual teacher, I would begin by putting the cost of the seminar into the cost box. Then I would add in additional needed expenses such as gas, travel time, lodging, food, etc. With each cost addition the size of the cost box would grow.

Then I would assess the items that would go into my value box. With the addition of each item the size of the box would grow proportionately to the value of the item added. If for instance, I was going to be learning something I could learn no other place, that would expand the size of the value box greatly. In comparison, if I could stay at home and not need to travel to another city, that would be a value for sure, but it would expand the size of the value box only slightly.

The biggest value to be put in the value box would be the worth of the information and enlightenment I would potentially receive. The reality is that the 'enlightened teachings' passed on by many highfalutin gurus at very high prices, is the same information available for free or a very small charge from other spiritual teachers. To get around this inconvenient reality, many fake gurus will come up with something to offer they feel is original and enticing, such as attend their seminar and have your "DNA recoded to a higher level." Promotion of lofty, expensive, experiences or outcomes, without any proof of validity or real life, real time benefit, should be approached cautiously.

This is not to say a teacher should not charge to impart wisdom it probably took them years and some expense to gain, as well as expense to make available to the public in one form or another. Most people do not value that which they get for free and a reciprocation energy is important. Money is the easiest way to create the reciprocation energy in exchange for knowledge imparted. It just needs to be a reasonable amount meant to be an exchange for the true value and not merely a vehicle to enrich the guru. Some real-life occurrences have been particularly blatant. If you see the guru driving around in a fleet of Rolls Royce cars while the followers are begging for money at airports, just common sense should warn you that something is not right with that equation.

2. Humility vs. Egocentric

True spiritual teachers are humble, often very humble. They desire attention to be drawn to their message, not to them. False teachers are just the opposite. The message is secondary to them. They promote themselves first and their message second. In the truly warped cases they promote themselves first, second and third, and their message a distant fourth. Some refer to themselves in their promotional literature as 'Enlightened Masters", "Self-realized yogis", "a Saint", and in extreme cases, even encourage their followers to think of them as the "incarnation of Christ."

Being truly enlightened instills a tremendous sense of humility, a realization that for all we know, have learned and have grown, it is infinitesimal to all there still is to know, learn and grow. It also engenders a sense of stewardship, to do everything one can to help our fellow brothers and sisters on the upward path. Not for recognition or great financial reward, but simply because we love them as our brothers and sisters of life.

3. Self-Perception of Perfection

False teachers often see themselves as nearly perfect, as they impart their perceived wisdom to the imperfect mortal masses. They can react strongly to even the slightest criticism and have almost a complete inability to look inward and find areas for their own improvement, let alone correction of weaknesses or mistakes. Some of these 'Enlightened Masters', have even gone so far as to file lawsuits against any individuals audacious enough to question their motives, teachings or honesty.

4. The End-all of Enlightenment

Some spiritual teachers harp on 'enlightenment' as the great end-all goal of life. They can fill an entire day of speaking, or write a book about 'enlightenment', without ever actually telling you specifically how to take realistic steps within the hustle and bustle of your everyday life, to become more enlightened. And if you did by some miracle become more 'enlightened' on your own, what that actually means, or how it will benefit you is seldom clearly defined. However, you are always encouraged to 'feel' and 'believe' that the fact that you are seeking to become more 'enlightened', by attending their lecture or ascribing to their teachings, shows you are already moving upward and expanding.

5. Do As I Say, Not As I Do

Hypocrisy is an easy warning sign to see. Many gurus and 'enlightened teachers', preach one thing, but in their own lives, live another. They preach love and harmony, but have gone through three divorces. They teach that daily meditation is vital, but it seems to no longer be applicable to them. They preach the sanctity of all life, then order a dead cow, pig, or chicken cooked for dinner. They teach to live modestly and within your means, but they live in a mansion built on the sacrifices of their followers. There is no excuse for a person that purports to be a spiritual teacher to not be able to '*practice what they preach*.'

6. Focus On Materialistic Desires And Instant Gratification

The ways of the world are money, sex, and power and authority over others. Neophytes on the spiritual path are still tied to those urges. Any purported guru or spiritual teacher, no matter how acclaimed, who is still focused on any or all of those three ways of the world, have not yet truly embarked upon a higher spiritual path and hence have no ability to teach a path of greater light to others.

We live in a very materialistic, instant gratification world and the allure of any teacher that promises to help you to use 'laws of attraction' to become a magnet for money, sex, power and abundance, has a strong appeal as these are primal desires. There is absolutely nothing wrong with someone overtly seeking greater money, sex, power or abundance. The problem only arises when it is construed as somehow being a 'spiritual' path. Anyone that teaches that pursuit of the material things of the world is spiritual in nature, needs to be given a wide berth if you are truly interested in growing on a spiritual path.

7. Selfishness

A hallmark of any truly spiritual person regardless of their spiritual path, is a selflessness that is ever looking for ways to help others and bring joy to other peoples life, even if only a smile. And selflessness, by definition, is an act that neither desires or needs reward, compensation or anything more than the satisfaction of seeing that something you did brought happiness to another person. If the life of a guru or 'enlightened' teacher exhibits the opposite- always seeking financial or other reward for every act, and seldom just giving of their time out of love and caring; take the warning sign for what it is telling- this teacher has not yet found the higher path of light themselves. Selflessness, not selfishness, is a frequently seen and dominant trait of every spiritually advanced individual.

8. Promising Fast Growth In Exchange For Lots Of Dollars

A common misconception encouraged by the adage, "you get what you pay for", is that high priced seminars and retreats are going to affect major beneficial changes. It has to be true right? Otherwise why would it cost so much money? There certainly can be multiple benefits from workshops that last several days to a couple of weeks. Events that involve travel to other countries, for those who can afford such luxuries, can have additional cultural and spiritual benefits.

While spiritual growth may be jump started in such workshops, a teacher promoting 'self-actualization', or 'breakthrough enlightenment', or 'spiritual ascendance', from attendance at the $1000.00+ seminar or retreat, has greatly discounted the necessity of the experiences of life's journey to attain all the promoted promises. There comes that 'instant gratification' urge rearing up again.

The reality is that 'spiritual growth' and 'enlightenment' are a life-long process, forged in the relationships and experiences of real life challenges. Wise teachings from those who have invested many years walking the path before us, can help us to

Wolf in Sheep's Clothing, Human

more clearly understand the principals and set our sights on the goals of self-improvement. There are no fast lanes, but there are paths with wonderful signposts that helps us stay on the upward path, put there by those who walked before us. Here's a great little poem I memorized long ago to remind me of the importance of heeding the guidance of humble teachers who have lived the life.

He stood at the crossroads all alone,
the sunlight in his face.
He had no thought for the world unknown;
he was set for a manly race.
But the road stretched east, and the road stretched west,
and the lad knew not which road was best.
He chose the road that led him down,
and he lost the race and victor's crown.
He was caught at last in an angry snare,
because no one had stood at the crossroads there
To show him the better way.

Another day, at this self-same place,
another lad with high hopes stood.
He too was set for a manly race;
he too was seeking the things which are good.
But one was there that the roads did know,
and this one showed him which way to go.
The lad turned away from the road that would have led
him down,
and he won the race and the victor's crown.
Today he walks the highways fair,
because one stood at the crossroads there,
and showed him a better way.

Chapter 24

PREDATORY ENERGY VAMPIRES

Please reread Chapter 16, on *Regretful Energy Vampires*. Predatory Energy Vampires have all the same warped needs to suck Soul Essence energy from people during conflicts as the regretful version. The difference, is they are very aware it is a need, and they not only do not feel bad about preying energetically on others, they actually look forward to it. They strive to create situations of conflict where they can feed on the negative energy.

Serial killers become the worst manifestation of predator Energy Vampires. The fear that people experience as they are tormented, injured, then finally killed, is so craved by the worst of the Energy Vampires that one murder just leads to the next, as they develop an insatiable lust for the palpable fear and terror of their victims.

The same defenses outlined for the unintentional Energy Vampires apply to the predators. Even greater emphasis should be placed on complete and total avoidance, carried out as soon as possible, with no looking back. Even if this is a close family member or spouse, permanently leaving the relationship and the state or country if necessary, should be done without delay.

If you are in the unfortunate situation to be in the relationship with a Predatory Energy Vampire that you cannot at the moment escape from, institute as much of the 4 step treatment plan outlined in Chapter 16 as possible, even if done without the knowledge or consent of the vampire. These protections won't completely stop attacks, but they will lessen their frequency and severity.

If you are in a life-threatening situation living with a Predatory Energy Vampire and have no means to leave, as a last resort you can seek out an Adept of Celestine Vibronics or Celestine Light, or a very experienced witch. In addition to the four active measures you can take yourself, an Adept can create a powerful Ward so at the very least, when you are within its protective space, the negative energy of the vampire will be repelled and refocused elsewhere. There are even more severe counter actions an Adept could institute. But its best left between you and them to describe and decide if you need them.

The 3 Types Of Negative Energy People

It is helpful to review the 3 types of people that embody negative energy that you will encounter in your life and the differing means to deal with them.

The first type, as discussed in Chapter 12, are people that are good people, desiring good things for themselves and others, but happen to exude a negative energy that depresses others when they are around them. Sometimes they affect all people. Others only affect certain people whose own auric energy is very discordant with theirs. Many of the negative energy people are aware of the depressing effect they have on other people and they often desperately desire someone to help them.

The good news is that a professional who works with energy, such as a Celestine Vibronics Adept, can help them and permanently cure their problem. And as outlined in Chapter 12, they can probably help themselves as well, or use your help to alleviate their chaotic energy dilemma. And even at its worst, though they are affecting your energy they are not drawing energy from you as a vampire does.

The second type are the Regretful Energy Vampires. Sadly, arguments and confrontations with Energy Vampires of any variety do suck energy from your Soul Essence. Though the

Predatory Energy Vampires

safest course is to just walk out of the life of any Energy Vampire, accommodation can be obtained with the regretful variety if they are willing to apply the methods outlined in Chapter 16. Long-term fulfilling relationships are still possible with any that fully embrace the treatment.

The third type are the Predatory Energy Vampires. There is nothing you can do to change them from their path, because it is one they fully desire and even crave. However, a very useful skill to develop is to learn to clearly see auras, so you can immediately identify Energy Vampires when you encounter them. My book *Auras: How to See, Feel & Know*, and my book *Unleash Your Psychic Powers*, can both be very helpful in assisting your development of your auric abilities.

CONCLUSION

I know this book will make some people uncomfortable. It always easier to not have to look at the dark side of life. But it is there, especially so in the world of the paranormal. Ignoring the reality may give one a false sense of bliss and security, but it doesn't change the reality. Most people will never need much in the way of psychic self-defense. It is not like there are threats abounding. But should they show up, I hope you have learned a few of the lessons imparted herein and are prepared.

There is a great added benefit as well. As you study and practice your psychic self-defense skills, you will be strengthening and improving all of your psychic abilities and paranormal powers. Practicing anything of a psychic or paranormal nature works and builds all of your psychic and paranormal muscles. In the long run your psychic development will grow faster, and your everyday life will be safer and more rewarding at the same time.

Go in your light, with love & joy,

Embrosewyn

PS If you enjoyed and benefited from this book, please be kind and leave a nice review for it on Amazon.

OTHER CAPTIVATING, THOUGHT-PROVOKING BOOKS BY EMBROSEWYN

CELESTINE LIGHT MAGICKAL SIGILS OF HEAVEN AND EARTH

What would happen if you could call upon the blessings of angels and amplify their miracles with the pure essence of spiritual magick?

Miracles manifest! That is the exciting reality that awaits you in *Celestine Light Magickal Sigils of Heaven and Earth*.

Calling upon the higher realm power of angels, through intentional summoning using specific magickal sigils and incantations, is considered to be the most powerful magick of all. But there is a magickal method even greater. When you combine calling upon a mighty angel with adding synergistic sigils and words of power, the amplification of the magickal energy can be astounding and the results that are manifested truly miraculous. This higher technique of magick is the essence of *Celestine Light Magickal Sigils of Heaven and Earth*.

This is the third book of the Magickal Celestine Light series and is an intermediate level reference book for students and practitioners of Celestine Light Magick. It contains a melding of the sigils and names of 99 of the 144 Angels found in *Angels of Miracles and Manifestation*, coupled with synergistic sigils and magickal incantations found within *Words of Power and Transformation*. To fully be able to implement the potent combination of angel magick and words of power magick revealed in this book, the practitioner should have previously read and have available as references the earlier two books in the series.

When magickal incantations and their sigils are evoked

in conjunction with the summoning of an angel for a focused purpose, the magickal results are often exceptional. The potent combination of calling upon angels and amplifying your intent with words of power and sigils of spiritual magick creates an awesome, higher magickal energy that can manifest everyday miracles. Employing this potent form of magick can convert challenges into opportunities, powerfully counter all forms of negative magick, entities, phobias, fears and people, greatly enhance good fortune, and help change ordinary lives into the extraordinary.

ANGELS OF MIRACLES AND MANIFESTATION
144 Names, Sigils and Stewardships To Call the Magickal Angels of Celestine Light

You are not alone. Whatever obstacle or challenge you face, whatever threat or adversary looms before you, whatever ability you seek to gain or mountain of life you want to conquer, divine angelic help is ready to intervene on your behalf. When the unlimited power of magickal angels stand with you, obstacles become opportunities, low times become springboards for better days, relationships blossom, illness becomes wellness, challenges become victories and miracles happen!

In *Angels of Miracles and Manifestation*, best-selling spiritual, magickal and paranormal author Embrosewyn Tazkuvel, reveals the secrets to summoning true magickal angels. And once called, how to use their awesome divine power to transform your compelling needs and desires into manifested reality.

Angel magick is the oldest, most powerful and least understood of all methods of magick. Ancient books of scripture from multiple religions tell of the marvelous power and miracles of angels. But the secrets of the true angel names, who they really are, their hierarchy, their stewardship responsibilities, their sigils, and how to successfully call them and have them work their divine magick for you, was lost to the world as a large part of it descended into the dark ages.

But a covenant was made by the Archangel Maeádael to the Adepts of Magick that as the people of the world evolved to a higher light the knowledge and power of angels would come again to the earth during the time of the Generation of Promise. That time is now. We are the Generation of Promise that has been foretold of for millennium. And all that was lost has been restored.

It doesn't matter what religion or path of enlightenment and empowerment that you travel: Wicca, Christianity, Pagan, Jewish, Buddhist, Occult, Muslim, Kabbalah, Vedic, something else or none at all. Nor does your preferred system of magick from Enochian, Thelemic, Gardnerian, Hermetic, to Tantric matter. Once you know the true names of the mighty angels, their unique sigils, and the simple but specific way to summon them, they will come and they will help you.

This revealing book of the ancient Celestine Light magick gives you immediate access to the divine powers of 14 Archangels, 136 Stewardship Angels, and hundreds of Specialty Angels that serve beneath them. Whether you are a novice or a magickal Adept you will find that when angels are on your side you manifest results that you never imagined possible except in your dreams.

The angel magick of Celestine Light is simple and direct without a lot of ritual, which makes it easy even for the novice to be able to quickly use it and gain benefit. While there is a place and importance to ritual in other types of magickal conjuring it is not necessary with angels. They are supernatural beings of unlimited power and awareness whose stewardship includes responding quickly to people in need who call upon them. You do not need elaborate rituals to get their attention.

If you are ready to have magick come alive in your life; if you are ready for real-life practical results that bring wisdom, happiness, health, love and abundance; if you are ready to unveil your life's purpose and unleash your own great potential, obtain the treasure that is this book. Call upon the magickal angels and they will come. But be prepared. When you summon angels, the magick happens and it is transformative. Your life will improve in ways big and small. But it will never be the same.

Want to know more? Take a moment to click on the Look Inside tab in the upper left of this page to see the full extent of the marvels that await you inside this book!

WORDS OF POWER AND TRANSFORMATION
101+ Magickal Words and Sigils of Celestine Light To Manifest Your Desires

Whatever you seek to achieve or change in your life, big or small, Celestine Light magickal words and sigils can help your sincere desires become reality.

Drawing from an ancient well of magickal power, the same divine source used by acclaimed sorcerers, witches and spiritual masters through the ages, the 101+ magickal words and sigils are revealed to the public for the very first time. They can create quick and often profound improvements in your life.

It doesn't matter what religion you follow or what you believe or do not believe. The magickal words and sigils are like mystical keys that open secret doors regardless of who holds the key. If you put the key in and turn it, the door will open and the magick will swirl around you!

From the beginner to the Adept, the Celestine Light words of power and sigils will expand your world and open up possibilities that may have seemed previously unachievable. Everything from something simple like finding a lost object, to something powerful like repelling a psychic or physical attack, to something of need such as greater income, to something life changing like finding your Soul Mate.

Some may wonder how a few spoken words combined with looking for just a moment at a peculiar image could have such immediate and often profound effects. The secret is these are ancient magick words of compelling power and the sigils are the embodiment of their magickal essence. Speaking or even thinking the words, or looking at or even picturing the sigil in your mind, rapidly draws angelic and magickal energies to you like iron to a magnet to fulfill the worthy purpose you desire.

This is a book of potent white magick of the light. Without a lot of training or ritual, it gives you the ability to overcome darkness threatening you from inside or out. For what is darkness except absence of the light? When light shines, darkness fades and disappears, not with a roar, but with a whimper.

Use the words and sigils to call in the magickal energies to transform and improve your life in every aspect. In this comprehensive book you will find activators to propel your personal growth, help you excel in school, succeed in your own business, or launch you to new heights in your profession. It will give you fast acting keys to improve your relationships, change your luck, revitalize your health, and develop and expand your psychic abilities.

Embrosewyn Tazkuvel is an Adept of the highest order in Celestine Light. After six decades of using magick and teaching it to others he is now sharing some of the secrets of what he knows with you. Knowledge that will instantly connect you to divine and powerful universal forces that with harmonic resonance, will unleash the magickal you!

Inside you will discover:

- 101 word combinations that call in magickal forces like a whirlwind of light.

- 177 magickal words in total.

- 101 sigils to go with each magickal word combination to amplify the magickal results you seek.

- 101 audio files you can listen to; helping you have perfect pronunciation of the Words of Power regardless of your native language. Available directly from the eBook and with a link in the paperback edition.

AURAS
How To See, Feel & Know

***Auras: How to See, Feel & Know*, is like three books in one!**

1. It's an information packed, full color, complete training manual with 17 time tested exercises and 47 photos and illustrations to help you quickly be able to see Auras in vibrant color! It is the only full color book on auras available.

2. An entertaining read as Embrosewyn recalls his early childhood and high school experiences seeing auras, and the often humorous reactions by everyone from his mother to his friends when he told them what he saw.

3. Plus, a fascinating chapter on body language. Embrosewyn teaches in his workshops to not just rely on your interpretation of the aura alone, but to confirm it with another indicator such as body language. *Auras: How to See, Feel & Know*, goes in depth with thorough explanations and great pictures to show you all the common body language indicators used to confirm what someone's aura is showing you.

Auras includes:
- 17 dynamic eye exercises to help you rapidly begin to see the beautiful world of auras!
- 47 full color pictures and illustrations (in the Kindle or Full Color print edition).

Anyone with vision in both eyes can begin seeing vividly colored auras around any person with just 5 minutes of practice!

Learn how to:
- See the 7 layers of the aura using Embrosewyn's pioneering technique
- Understand the meaning of the patterns and shadows observed in the layers
- Train your eyes to instantly switch back and forth from aura to normal vision
- Understand the meaning and nuances of every color of

the rainbow in an aura
- Use your aura as a shield against negative energy or people
- Power up your aura to have greater achievement in any endeavor
- Interpret body language to confirm observations of the aura
- Cut negative energy cords to disharmonious people
- Understand health conditions and ailments through the aura

The secret to aura sight is to retrain the focusing parts of your eyes to see things that have always been there, but you have never been able to see before. It's really not complicated. Anyone can do it using Embrosewyn's proven techniques and eye exercises. The author has been seeing brightly colored auras for over 60 years and teaching others to begin seeing auras within 5 minutes for the last 22 years. *Auras: How to See, Feel & Know*, includes all the power techniques, tools and Full Color eye exercises from his popular workshops.

For those who already have experience seeing auras, the deeper auric layers and subtle auric nuances and the special ways to focus your eyes to see them, are explained in detail, with Full Color pictures andillustrations to show you how the deeper layers and auric aberrations appear. It is also a complete training manual to help you quickly be able to see Auras in vibrant color. It includes 17 eye exercises and dozens of Full Color pictures, enabling anyone with vision in both eyes to begin seeing vividly colored auras around any person. The secret is in retraining the focusing parts of your eyes to see things that have always been there, but you have never been able to see before. *Auras: How to See, Feel & Know*, includes all the power techniques, tools and Full Color eye exercises from Embrosewyn's popular workshops.

Additionally, there is a fascinating chapter on body language. Embrosewyn teaches in his workshops to not just rely on your interpretation of the aura alone, but to confirm it with another indicator such as body language. *Auras: How to See, Feel & Know* goes in depth with thorough explanations and great pictures to show you all the common body language indicators used to confirm what someone's aura is showing you.

For those who already have experience seeing auras, the deeper auric layers and subtle auric nuances and the special ways to focus your eyes to see them, are explained in detail, with accompanying Full Color pictures to show you how the deeper layers and auric aberrations appear.

SOUL MATE AURAS
How To Find Your Soul Mate & Happily Ever After

The romantic dream of finding your Soul Mate, the person with whom you resonate on every level of your being, is more than a wishful notion. It is a deeply embedded, primal desire that persists on some level despite what may have been years of quiet, inner frustration and included relationships that while fulfilling on some levels, still fell short of the completeness of a Soul Mate.

Once found, your relationship with your Soul Mate can almost seem like a dream at times. It will be all you expected and probably much more. Having never previously had a relationship that resonated in harmony and expansiveness on every level of your being, you will have had nothing to prepare you for its wonder. Having never stood atop a mountain that tall with an expansiveness so exhilarating, once experienced, a committed relationship with your Soul Mate will give you a bliss and fulfillment such as you probably only imagined in fairy tales.

But how to find your Soul Mate? That is the million dollar question. The vast majority of people believe finding your Soul Mate is like a magnetic attraction, it will somehow just happen; in some manner you'll just be inevitably drawn to each other. The harsh reality is, 99% of people realize by their old age that it never happened. Or, if it did occur they didn't recognize their Soul Mate at the time, because they were looking for a different ideal.

Soul Mate Auras: How To Find Your Soul Mate & Happily Ever After gives you the master keys to unlock the passageway to discovering your Soul Mate using the certainty of your auric connections. Every person has a unique aura and auric field generated by their seven energy centers and their vitality. Find the person that you resonate strongly with on all seven energy centers and you'll find your Soul Mate!

Everyone can sense and see auras. In *Soul Mate Auras* full color eye and energy exercises will help you learn how to see and feel auras and how to use that ability to identify where in the great big world your Soul Mate is living. Once you are physically in the presence of your prospective Soul Mate, you will know how to use your aura to energetically confirm that they are the one. The same methods can be used to discover multiple people that are Twin Flames with you; not quite seven auric connection Soul Mates, but still deep and expansive connections to you on five to six energy centers.

Soul Mate Auras also includes an in-depth procedure to determine if someone is a Twin Flame or Soul Mate, not by using your aura, but by honestly and rationally evaluating your connections on all seven of your energy centers. This is an invaluable tool for anyone contemplating marriage or entering a long-term committed relationship. It also serves as a useful second opinion confirmation for anyone that has used their aura to find their Soul Mate.

To help inspire and motivate you to create your own "happily ever after," *Soul Mate Auras* is richly accentuated with dozens of full color photos of loving couples along with profound quotes from famous to anonymous people about the wonder of Soul Mates.

Treat yourself to the reality of finding your Soul Mate or confirming the one that you have already found! Scroll to the upper left of the page and click on Look Inside to find out more about what's inside this book!

Secret Earth Series

INCEPTION
BOOK 1

Could it be possible that there is a man alive on the Earth today that has been here for two thousand years? How has he lived so long? And why? What secrets does he know? Can his knowledge save the Earth or is it doomed?

Continuing the epic historical saga begun in the *Oracles of Celestine Light*, but written as a novel rather than a chronicle, *Inception* unveils the life and adventures of Lazarus of Bethany and his powerful and mysterious sister Miriam of Magdala.

The first book of the Secret Earth series, *Inception*, reveals the hidden beginnings of the strange, secret life of Lazarus. From his comfortable position as the master of caravans to Egypt he is swept into a web of intrigue involving his enigmatic sister Miriam and a myriad of challenging dangers that never seem to end and spans both space and time.

Some say Miriam is an angel, while others are vehement that she is a witch. Lazarus learns the improbable truth about his sister, and along with twenty-three other courageous men and women, is endowed with the secrets of immortality. But he learns that living the secrets is not as easy as knowing them. And living them comes at a price; one that needs to be paid in unwavering courage, stained with blood, built with toil, and endured with millenniums of sacrifice, defending the Earth from all the horrors that might have been. *Inception* is just the beginning of their odyssey.

DESTINY
BOOK 2

In preparation, before beginning their training as immortal Guardians of the Earth, Lazarus of Bethany and his wife Hannah were asked to go on a short visit to a world in another dimension. "Just to look around a bit and get a feel for the differences," Lazarus's mysterious sister, Miriam of Magdala assured them.

She neglected to mention the ravenous monstrous birds, the ferocious fire-breathing dragons, the impossibly perfect people with sinister ulterior motives, and the fact that they would end up being naked almost all the time! And that was just the beginning of the challenges!

UNLEASH YOUR PSYCHIC POWERS

A Comprehensive 400 Page Guidebook

Unleash Your Psychic Powers is an entertaining, enlightening and educational resource for all levels of practitioners in the psychic, magickal and paranormal arts. It includes easy-to-follow, step-by-step instructions on how you can develop and enhance the full potential of dynamic psychic, magickal and paranormal powers in your own life.

Whether You Are A Novice Or An Adept

You will find valuable insight and guidance, based upon Embrosewyn's six decades of experience discovering and developing psychic and paranormal talents and unleashing the power of the magickal arts.

Twenty Psychic And Paranormal Abilities Are Explored

Including well known abilities such as Clairvoyance, Telekinesis, Telepathy, Lucid Dreaming, Precognition, Astral Projection and Faith Healing, plus, more obscure talents such as Channeling, Dowsing, and Automatic Handwriting.

In addition to helping you develop and master the psychic abilities that call to you, each of the twenty powers described are spiced with fascinating personal stories from the lives of Embrosewyn and others, to help you understand some of the real world consequences and benefits of using these formidable magickal and psychic talents. Paranormal abilities have saved Embrosewyn's life and the lives of his family members on multiple occasions. Learning to fully develop your own psychic and paranormal abilities may come in just as handy one day.

For anyone that is an active spirit medium, or uses any psychic abilities involving other-worldly beings, such as divination, channeling, or ghost hunting, the chapter on Psychic Self-defense is an extensive must read, covering low, medium and high risk threats, including everything from negative vortexes, to entities, energy vampires, ghosts, aliens and demons. Exorcism, and how to protect both people and property from unseen forces is also completely explained.

Filled with pictures and vivid descriptions of how you can bring forth and develop your own transcendental supernatural gifts, *Unleash Your Psychic Powers* should be in the library of every serious student of the psychic, magickal, paranormal and supernatural.

Everyone has psychic and paranormal abilities. It is your birthright! You were born with them!

Within this book you'll learn how to unlock and unleash your astounding supernatural potential and the amazing things you can do with your powers once they are free!

PSYCHIC SELF DEFENSE

A Complete Guide to Protecting Yourself Against Psychic & Paranormal Attack (and just plain irksome people)

Felt a negative energy come over you for no apparent reason when you are near someone or around certain places? Had a curse hurled at you? Spooked by a ghost in a building? Imperiled by demonic forces? Being drained and discombobulated by an energy vampire? Or, do you encounter more mundane but still disruptive negative energies like an over demanding boss, the local bully, hurtful gossip, a physically or mentally abusive spouse, or life in a dangerous neighborhood threatened by thieves and violence? Whatever your source of negative energy, danger or threat, you'll find effective, proven, psychic and magickal countermeasures within this book.

Psychic Self Defense draws upon Embrosewyn's six decades of personal experience using psychic abilities and magickal defenses to thwart, counter and send back to sender, any and all hostile paranormal threats. Everything from unsupportive and dismissive family and friends, to ghosts, demons and exorcisms. The same practical and easy to learn Magickal techniques can be mastered by anyone serious enough to give it some time and practice, and can aid you immensely with a host of material world challenges as well.

17 psychic and paranormal threats are covered with exact, effective counter measures, including many real life examples from Embrosewyn's comprehensive personal experiences with the paranormal, devising what works and what doesn't from hard won trial and error.

Whether you are a medium needing to keep foul spirits away, or simply someone desiring to know that you, your family and property are safe and protected, you will find the means to insure peace and security with the proven methods outlined in *Psychic Self Defense*

You will learn how to:

- Create your own Magick spells tailored to your particular situation and need
- Call upon specific angels to aid you
- Create Crystal Energy Shields
- Protect yourself when in a channeling or spirit medium trance
- Use your Aura to create ASP's (Auric Shields of Power)
- Empower Wards for protection against specific threats
- Recognize and counter Energy Vampires
- Cleanse a home of negative energy
- Cut negative energy cords to disharmonious people
- Counter Black Magick
- Detect alien presence
- Banish malicious entities or demons

Though dealing with numerous and sometimes dangerous other-worldly and material world threats, the entire approach of this book is from a position of personal empowerment, no fear, and divine white light. Whether you are religious or an atheist, an experienced practitioner of the psychic and magickal arts or a neophyte, someone living in a haunted house or just an employee wanting to have a nicer boss, there will be hundreds of ways you can use the information in this book to help you in your life. And you will learn to do it in ways that are uplifting and empowering, producing results that are peaceful, safe and harmonious.

Psychic Self Defense is also available as an AUDIO BOOK.

22 STEPS TO THE LIGHT OF YOUR SOUL

A Treasured Book That Will Help You Unleash The Greatness Within

What would it be like if you could reach through space and time to query the accumulated wisdom of the ages and get an answer? 22 Steps to the Light of Your Soul, reveals such treasured insights, eloquently expounding upon the foundational principles of 22 timeless subjects of universal interest and appeal, to help each reader grow and expand into their fullest potential.

In a thought-provoking, poetic writing style, answers to questions we all ponder upon, such as love, happiness, success and friendship, are explored and illuminated in short, concise chapters, perfect for a thought to ponder through the day or contemplate as your eyes close for sleep.

Each paragraph tells a story and virtually every sentence could stand alone as an inspiring quote on your wall.

These are the 22 steps of the Light of Your Soul
Step 1: The Purpose of Life
Step 2: Balance
Step 3: Character
Step 4: Habits
Step 5: Friendship
Step 6: True Love
Step 7: Marriage
Step 8: Children
Step 9: Happiness
Step 10: Play & Relaxation
Step 11: Health
Step 12: Success
Step 13: Knowledge
Step 14: Passion & Serenity
Step 15: Imagination & Vision
Step 16: Creativity & Art

Step 17: Adversity
Step 18: Respect
Step 19: Freedom & Responsibility
Step 20: Stewardship
Step 21: Faith
Step 22: Love Yourself - the Alpha and the Omega

ALSO AVAILABLE AS AN AUDIO BOOK! You can listen as you commute to work or travel on vacation, or even listen and read together!

LOVE YOURSELF
The Secret Key to Transforming Your Life

Loving yourself is all about energy

As humans we devote a great deal of our energy through our time, thoughts and emotions to love. We read about it, watch movies and shows about it, dream about it, hope for it to bless our lives, feel like something critically important is lacking when it doesn't, and at the very least keep a sharp eye out for it when its missing.

Too often we look to someone else to fulfill our love and crash and burn when relationships end, or fail to live up to our fantasies of what we thought they should be. When we seek love from another person or source greater than the love we give to ourselves, we set ourselves up to an inevitable hard landing when the other person or source ceases to provide the level of fulfillment we desire.

Loving yourself is a precious gift from you to you. It is an incredibly powerful energy that not only enhances your ability to give love more fully to others, it also creates a positive energy of expanding reverberation that brings more love, friendship and appreciation to you from all directions. It is the inner light that illuminates your life empowering you to create the kind of life you desire and dream.

The relationship you have with yourself is the most important one in your life. Happiness will forever be fleeting if you do not have peace, respect and love for yourself. It's not selfish. It's not vain. It is in fact the key to transforming your life. Inward reflection and appreciation will open up clearer channels to the divine. Relationships with everyone will be enhanced as your relationship with yourself expands and is uplifted.

All other relationships are only mirrors of the one you have within. As you love yourself, are kind to yourself, respect yourself, so too will you be able to give those and so many other good qualities to others in equal measure to that which you give to yourself.

This is a short, but very sweet book to help you discover your inner glow of love. Within its covers are two great keys you will find no other place. These two keys will proactively bring you to the serenity of self-love regardless of whether you are currently near or far from that place of peace.

Are you familiar with the infinity symbol? It looks pretty much like the number 8 turned on its side. As love for yourself should be now and forever, in the last chapter you will find 88 reasons why loving yourself is vitally important to your joy, personal growth and expansion, and the happiness of everyone whose lives you touch. Most people have never considered that there could be a list that long just about loving yourself! But with each short phrase you read your mind begins to understand to a greater depth how important loving yourself is for all aspects of your life and relationships. As your mind understands your life follows.

This book leaves you with a special gift Inside you'll find two short, but very valuable multimedia flash presentations. One is entitled "Forgive Yourself". The other is "Love Yourself." These are not normal flash presentations. They are self-hypnosis, positive affirmations that will rapidly help you achieve greater self-love and more fulfilling love-filled realities in your life. As soft repetitive music plays in the background, images reinforcing the theme will flash by on your screen about three per second, accompanied by short phrases superimposed on a portion of the image. In a quick 7-10 minute session, sitting at home in front of your computer, you will find the flash presentations buoy and motivate you. Repeat them twice a day for several days and you will find they are transformative.

Special Bonus: *Love Yourself* is ALSO AVAILABLE AS AN AUDIO BOOK! This allows you to listen and read at the same time!

ORACLES OF CELESTINE LIGHT
Complete Trilogy Of Genesis, Nexus & Vivus

Once in a lifetime comes a book that can dramatically change your life for the better - forever. This is it!

WHAT WAS LOST...HAS BEEN FOUND

This is the complete 808 page trilogy of the Celestine books of Light: Genesis, Nexus and Vivus.

The controversial *Oracles of Celestine Light*, is a portal in time to the days of Yeshua of Nazareth, over 2000 years ago, revealed in fulfilling detail to the world by the reclusive Embrosewyn Tazkuvel. It includes 155 chapters of sacred wisdom, miracles and mysteries revealing life-changing knowledge about health, longevity, happiness and spiritual expansion that reverberates into your life today.

Learn the startling, never before understood truth:

About aliens, other dimensions, Atlantis, Adam & Eve, the Garden of Eden, Noah and the ark, giants, the empowerment of women, dreams, angels, Yeshua of Nazareth (Jesus), his crucifixion & resurrection, his wife Miriam of Magdala (Mary Magdala), Yudas Iscariot (Judas), the afterlife, reincarnation, energy vortexes, witches, magic, miracles, paranormal abilities, and you!

The **Or***acles of Celestine Light* turns accepted religious history and traditional teachings on their head. But page by page, it makes more sense than anything you've ever read and shares simple yet profound truths to make your life better today and help you to understand and unleash your miraculous potential.

The *Oracles of Celestine Light* explains who you are, why you are here, and your divine destiny. It is a must-read for anyone interested in spirituality, personal growth and thought-provoking answers to the unknown.

"You are a child of God, a Child of Light, literally a priceless son or daughter of divinity. Even through the fog of mortal upheavals and the tumults and tribulations, always remember you are still a child of God and shall inherit joy and kingdoms beyond measure, as you remain true to your light." Genesis 11:99

Psychic Awakening Series
CLAIRVOYANCE

Would it be helpful if you could gain hidden knowledge about a person, place, thing, event, or concept, not by any of your five physical senses, but with visions and "knowing?"

Are you ready to supercharge your intuition? *Clairvoyance* takes you on a quest of self-discovery and personal empowerment, helping you unlock this potent ESP ability in your life. It includes riveting stories from Embrosewyn's six decades of psychic and paranormal adventures, plus fascinating accounts of others as they discovered and cultivated their supernatural abilities.

Clearly written, step-by-step practice exercises will help you to expand and benefit from your own psychic and clairvoyant abilities. This can make a HUGE improvement in your relationships, career and creativity. As Embrosewyn has proven from over twenty years helping thousands of students to find and develop their psychic and paranormal abilities, EVERYONE, has one or more supernatural gifts. *Clairvoyance* will help you discover and unleash yours!

If you are interested in helping yourself to achieve more happiness, better health, greater knowledge, increased wealth and a deeper spirituality, unlocking your power of clairvoyance can be the key. Hidden knowledge revealed becomes paths unseen unveiled.

Unleashing your psychic gifts does more than just give you advantage in life challenges. It is a safe, ethical, even spiritual and essential part of you that makes you whole, once you accept that you have these special psychic abilities and begin to use them.

TELEKINESIS

Easy, comprehensive guide for anyone wanting to develop the supernatural ability of Telekinesis

Telekinesis, also known as psychokinesis, is the ability to move or influence the properties of objects without physical contact. Typically it is ascribed as a power of the mind. But as Embrosewyn explains, based upon his sixty years of personal experience, the actual physical force that moves and influences objects emanates from a person's auric field. It initiates with a mental thought, but the secret to the power is in your aura!

Telekinesis is the second book in the Psychic Awakening series by popular paranormal writer Embrosewyn Tazkuvel. The series was specifically created to offer short, inexpensive, information filled handbooks to help you quickly learn and develop specific psychic and paranormal abilities.

Clearly written, *Telekinesis* is filled with step-by-step practice exercises and training techniques proven to help you unlock this formidable paranormal ability. Spiced with riveting accounts of real-life psychic experiences and paranormal adventures, you'll be entertained while you learn. But along the way you will begin to unleash the potent power of Telekinesis in your own life!

As Embrosewyn has proven from over twenty years helping thousands of students to find and develop their psychic and paranormal abilities. EVERYONE, has one or more supernatural gifts. Is Telekinesis one of yours? Perhaps it's time to find out.

DREAMS

Awaken in the world of your sleep

In *Dreams*, the third book of the Psychic awakening series, renowned psychic/paranormal practitioner Embrosewyn Tazkuvel reveals some of his personal experiences with the transformational effect of dreams, while sharing time-tested techniques and insights that will help you unlock the power of your own night travels.

Lucid Dreaming

An expanded section on Lucid Dreaming gives you proven methods to induce and develop your innate ability to control your dreams. It explores the astonishing hidden world of your dream state that can reveal higher knowledge, greatly boost your creativity, improve your memory, and help you solve vexing problems of everyday life that previously seemed to have no solution.

Nine Types of Dreams

Detailing the nine types of dreams will help you to understand which dreams are irrelevant and which you should pay close attention to, especially when they reoccur. You'll gain insight into how to interpret the various types of dreams to understand which are warnings and which are gems of inspiration that can change your life from the moment you awaken and begin to act upon that which you dreamed.

Become the master of your dreams

Sleeping and dreaming are a part of your daily life that cumulatively accounts for dozens of years of your total life. It is a valuable time of far more than just rest. Become the master of your dreams and your entire life can become more than you ever imagined possible. Your dreams are the secret key to your future.

Additional Services Offered by Embrosewyn
~ on a limited basis ~

I am honored to be able to be of further service to you by offering multiple paranormal abilities for your enlightenment and life assistance. On a limited basis as my time allows I can: discover your Soul Name and the meaning and powers of the sounds; custom craft and imbue enchantments upon a piece of your jewelry for a wide beneficial range of purposes; discover the name of your Guardian Angel; have an in-depth psychic consultation and Insight Card reading with you via a Skype video call. My wife Sumara can also create a beautiful piece of collage art on 20"x30" internally framed canvas, representing all of the meanings and powers of the sounds of your Soul Name.

If you are interested in learning more about any of these additional services please visit my website, *www.embrosewyn.com* and click on the link at the top for SERVICES.

Made in the USA
Middletown, DE
27 May 2018